YOU'RE HIRED !

COMPELLING COVERING LETTERS

**Liz Dinse
and Jude Hanley**

trotman | t

You're Hired! Compelling Covering Letters

This first edition published in 2024 by Trotman, an imprint of Trotman Indigo Publishing Ltd, 18e Charles Street, Bath BA1 1HX

© Trotman Indigo Publishing Ltd 2024

Authors: Liz Dinse and Jude Hanley

British Library Cataloguing in Publication Data
A catalogue record for this book is available from the British Library.

ISBN 978 1 911724 20 9

Every effort has been made to trace copyright holders and to obtain their permission for the use of copyright material. The publisher apologises for any errors or omissions, and would be grateful to be notified of any corrections that should be incorporated in future editions of this book.

Printed and bound in the UK by 4Edge Ltd, Hockley, Essex

All details in this book were correct at the time of going to press. To keep up-to-date with all the latest news and updates and to access the online resources that accompany this book, use the QR code or visit **trotman.co.uk/pages/ compelling-covering-letters-resources**

CONTENTS

ACKNOWLEDGEMENTS

Thank you to our always patient families: Lawrence, Nicky, Kyle and Noah, as well as the various members of the Careers Writers Association for their input, advice and support.

ABOUT THE AUTHORS

Liz Dinse is a member of the Careers Writers Association (CWA), a practising freelance careers coach, employment expert and writer. She holds a PhD in reflective practice and career guidance and has over 20 years' experience supporting disabled people. Between 2008 and 2022 she worked as a specialist disability careers adviser in higher education offering guidance to disabled university students and graduates. She is now a freelance careers professional specialising in disability and HE and an employment expert.

Liz is a member of the Association of Graduate Careers Advisory Services (AGCAS) and was part of its Disability Task Group. She is also a member of the Career Development Institute (CDI) and a Registered Career Development Professional (RCDP).

Liz has written for the National Institute for Career Education and Counselling (NICEC), *Phoenix* (the AGCAS journal) and *Career Matters* (Career Development Institute professional magazine).

Jude Hanley, member of the Careers Writers Association (CWA), is a freelance writer and practising Careers Adviser and Careers Leader. She has 30 years' experience working in schools, colleges and higher education, as well as with NEET young people.

Alongside working in a secondary school with a sixth form and freelance writing, Jude previously had her own careers consultancy business called Queer Careers. As an advocate of equality, diversity and inclusion (EDI) and a Stonewall LGBT Workplace Role Model she often writes about EDI topics.

Jude has had job profiles and articles published on prospects.ac.uk and created content for the Abintegro careers platform as well as the Careers Development Institute (CDI) publication, *Career Matters*. She most recently wrote an article about the use of Instagram in job searching.

INTRODUCTION

When applying for a job, it's possible that you'll be asked to submit a covering letter to accompany a CV or other documents. For some, this is something they have done before and are prepared for, but for other job seekers, it's a completely new challenge which they may or may not know how to approach.

On the face of it, writing a letter which is just a few hundred words long shouldn't be too difficult a task. But in reality, this letter needs to accomplish many things. It needs to persuade, inform and prove to an employer that the person who has written the letter is worthy of inviting in for an interview. If you hurriedly throw something together and hope for the best, the employer will be able to see this and get the impression that you aren't that serious about the role. Whereas, if it's obvious that you have put in the work to ensure you have submitted the best letter you can, the employer will respect that and carefully consider your application.

You're probably familiar with the saying 'first impressions count' and this is certainly true during the job application process. You may think this only comes into play when you are invited for an interview, and you meet the employer, but what the employer sees first from you is your covering letter. Therefore, it's important to give this short letter the time and attention it needs to make the best first impression. You've already made an excellent start by choosing to use this book to help you!

As you'll see from the book, it's not a case of one size fits all. We are all unique and can offer an employer many different things, so your covering letter needs to reflect this. Whether you're just finishing your education or you're already working and seeking a promotion, you'll find information here that will help you tailor your letter to whatever situation you need it for.

This book has been designed to take you through the process of planning and writing a covering letter step by step. It will cover topics such as understanding what a covering letter is, how to make effective use of AI, and how to share sensitive information, among others.

Throughout the book, you'll find example layouts and sentences to help illustrate the key points made in each chapter. You'll also find a list of additional resources which you can use to support you alongside this book.

We hope that this book assists you in writing a compelling covering letter and helps bring you success.

1 WHAT IS A COVERING LETTER?

In day-to-day life, fewer of us write a letter to someone these days. Most of us might have written an email to someone, that is, a friend, a colleague or an organisation, which is the start of a letter. You may not have thought of this as 'writing a letter' and may not have planned out your letter or given great thought to the contents.

So, what is a covering letter? The *Collins English Dictionary* (2024) notes that:

> a covering letter is a letter that you send with a parcel or with another letter in order to provide extra information.

Or, according to the *Cambridge Dictionary* (2024) it is:

> a letter that contains information about the thing it is sent with.

that is, please send a covering letter with your application form.

Therefore, your covering letter aims to provide extra information. It gives you a space to add some context to aspects of your CV. It is usually an A4-size document, typically three to five paragraphs long.

It is not meant to duplicate your CV. If you are unsure what to include in your covering letter, look at Chapter 2, 'Understanding What Should Be in Each Section'. Briefly, in your covering letter, you can 'introduce yourself', say 'why you', 'why them' and add any further information.

Why write one, and how it fits with your application

For many online applications, you must register and apply via the employer's job page. They ask you to complete the application and give details of your education, dates, qualifications and employment. Then, there is usually space to provide a personal statement explaining how you meet the job requirements and personal specifications. When an employer asks you to send them a CV, the CV gives the employer the facts, that is, dates and periods of education and employment. It does not give much space for anything else apart from the 'personal statement' or 'career aims' at the start of your CV, which is usually three or four lines long. Ultimately, your covering letter gives you the space to explain why you are the best applicant and allows you to show the employer you have researched them as an employer and organisation.

Typically, when employers ask you to send them your CV, they then ask you to support your application and provide further information by way of your covering letter; see below a few examples of job adverts requesting you to:

- send a covering letter explaining why you have applied and your chosen role (Raytheon UK, 2023);

- send a CV and covering letter outlining your interest and suitability for the role (St Andrews University).

Overall, the covering letter gives you an extra page to explain to the employer why you.

Remember, your letter gives the first impression of you, and it is your chance to stand out from the crowd. Here, you can then link what is on your CV to the criteria in the person specification, as well as introduce yourself, stating why you chose them as an employer and/ or organisation, why you are the best applicant and, importantly, you link your covering letter and CV together.

When to write one

If you are applying for a role that you have seen advertised, it is important to follow the instructions given by the employer; see below for a few examples from either job portals or external adverts.

To apply for this role, please submit the following:

- CV
- A personal statement that identifies how you meet the criteria in the person specification. Please ensure that you provide relevant examples as evidence to support your statements.
- Remember to attach your CV and Personal statement as ONE DOCUMENT (Open University Scotland, 2024).

The external advert for the following role as a business support coordinator does not mention a covering letter. However, upon registering on the job portal and looking in more detail at the requirements for the application, they require you to also:

- Upload your resume (CV) and add a covering letter (University of Edinburgh, 2024).

Other employers may say something like this:

- 'Cover Letter explaining why you have applied and your chosen role' (Raytheon UK, 2023).

Therefore, it is important to check what the employer is asking for before spending the time and effort writing something that might not be required, so check and double-check, especially if the application is through a job portal.

Overview of what you should include or avoid.

Usually, your covering letter should include:

- your contact details;
- employer's contact details;
- introduction to you and why you are writing;
- why you want to work for them;
- why you'd be the best person for the job;
- additional information;
- closing statement.

But, your covering letter should avoid:

- not reading and/or following the application instructions;
- statements that are not true;
- copying and pasting from a previously written covering letter or using a generic letter;
- writing a lengthy letter over multiple pages;

- repeating the same information as on your CV;

- using negative language and/or tone.

> *Remember – the recruiter may be trawling through many letters and CVs, so give them a reason to pause and place you on the shortlist. That is the goal of a compelling and effective covering letter. (Kathleen Houston, Career Coach and Senior Teaching Fellow)*

This chapter has outlined what a covering letter is and how it fits alongside your CV and application form. Remember that your letter provides the space to explain in more depth how and why you are the best applicant for the role. It is important not to write your covering letter as a stand-alone document or use a generic letter you have used multiple times. You need to tailor your letter to the job to get the best out of your application. As noted in the quote above, your letter needs to stand out; by creating a compelling covering letter, you increase your chances of being shortlisted. To gain a better understanding of how to tailor your letter, turn to Chapter 3, 'How to Tailor the Letter to the Job and Company'.

IN A NUTSHELL

- Check what the advert asks for, i.e. a CV and covering letter, or upload a CV and complete the personal statement section.

- Remember why you are writing the covering letter, i.e. to provide more information.

- Don't send a generic covering letter or overuse copy and paste.

- Include the basic ingredients, including introducing yourself, why you and why them.

2 UNDERSTANDING WHAT SHOULD BE IN EACH SECTION

Chapter 1 outlined what a covering letter is, when and why you need to write one, and provided an overview of what should and shouldn't be included. This chapter aims to help you better understand what to include in your letter. Sometimes, it's hard to think about the whole letter, so it is best to break your covering letter down into a few paragraphs. This chapter will help you consider what to include in these paragraphs. Before we get started, a reminder that it is as important to tailor your covering letter as it is to tailor your CV. Chapter 3, 'How to Tailor the Letter to the Job and Company', will help you to think about how to tailor your covering letter. If you need help tailoring your CV, look at *You're Hired! Standout CVs* by Corinne Mills (Trotman).

Many employers will note in their recruitment adverts that they wish you to apply, that is, with a CV and covering letter; see overleaf for a few examples:

- 'Cover Letter explaining why you have applied and your chosen role' (Raytheon UK, 2023).

- 'A cracking covering letter proving to us how good you are with words' (cgpbooks, 2023).

- In support of your application, please also include a combined Cover Letter & CV (St Andrews University).

- Send a CV and cover letter outlining your interest and suitability for the role (St Andrews University).

This is your opportunity to relate your experience to what a potential employer is looking for and to stand out from the crowd.

This chapter will help you:

- understand what information to include in your letter;

- understand what goes where, that is, paragraph 1 'the introduction';

- to layout your covering letter, including an example of a covering letter.

As you would have seen in Chapter 1, a covering letter usually is around three to five paragraphs long, and its basic ingredients are as follows:

- Your contact details.

- Employer contact details.

- Introduction to you and why you are writing.

- Why you'd be the best person for the job.

- Why you want to work for them.

- Additional Information.

- Closing statement.

If you are unsure what to include in each paragraph, here are more details.

Your contact details

If you are writing your letter in a Word document, you usually start by adding your name and contact details to the top right corner of your letter. You should include your name, address and contact information.

Address

When writing your covering letter, it is important to consider what you are using your covering letter for: that is, an application to an employer as part of an online application as additional supporting information. If this is the case, consider editing the contact details, as you may have added this information on the main application form. Regardless, check that you have included the correct contact details, and if you're a student, consider which details to include: that is, if you're studying and away from home, you may want to add your home and/or study address or make a note in the body of the letter stating where you will be living if you are offered the position.

Telephone numbers

These days, many of us change mobile phone contracts frequently, which could result in a number change. It is also important to check that you have given the correct telephone/mobile number. Also, ensure that you provide the number you are most likely to check regularly, which doesn't always ring to an answering service. This can be frustrating to a potential employer and could mean you miss out on an invitation to an interview.

Digital contact details

In the world of technology, a potential employer may contact you via email. Check that your email address is correct, and be mindful of which email address you include; it is best to use an email account that includes your name, for example, Olivia524 @hotmail.com, rather than an email address with a pet name or sports alliance, for example, footballmad@hotmail.com. Most of us now have social media accounts, such as, Facebook or Instagram; while you would not usually include these in your covering letter and CV, some sectors, such as the creative and film production sectors, are more inclined to use Instagram to post adverts and recruit new employees. It is wise to check your privacy settings and be mindful of posts in a world where anyone can Google you and view your profile. You should also consider adding your LinkedIn public profile link or URL; remember, you can edit this link to make it shorter simply by removing unnecessary numbers and letters. Otherwise, the link can look something like this: https://www.linked .com/Olivia524-8b66c2299. If you need help with how to do this, visit the Help pages on LinkedIn — Manage your public profile URL | LinkedIn Help.

Employer contact details

Once you have added your name, address and contact information, you must include the name and address of the person you are sending the letter to, usually on the left-hand side of the page. Ensure that you have their name spelt correctly and use the correct title (salutations) when writing a letter to a potential employer, that is, Mr, Ms, Mrs and so on. If you know the name of the person, then use this with their job title, followed by their address.

Introduction to you and why you are writing

Before you start the main body of your introduction, you usually add the date you wrote your letter and then a greeting, for example, Dear Mr Taylor. There are a variety of greetings you could use, including Hello and Hi, but these are considered somewhat informal so should be avoided when writing a covering letter.

If you do not know the name of the person you are addressing the letter to, you can add either Dear Hiring Manager, Recruitment Team, Creative Director, and so on, or 'To whom it may concern'. While in the past it was also common to add 'Dear Sir or Madam', it is important to note more gender-neutral introductions.

For more examples of how to address your letter or add pronouns, take a look at Chapter 9 'Digital versus Paper Letters'. Next, in the main body of the introduction, start by introducing yourself and explaining where you found the advert, for example, *Lancashire Evening Post* or Prospects.ac.uk, and so on; here, you can also add the job title or any reference number used in the advert.

Why you'd be the best person for the job

This is the paragraph where you state why you. It is important to highlight your relevant skills and experiences and tailor this section to the specific role you are applying for. If the advert states they require you to explain 'why you have applied to them and your chosen role', it is important to do this. Another application may ask for something different in the covering letter, that is, demonstrating you're good with words. This is why tailoring each covering letter and CV to each job application is important. Spend some time here reflecting on your skills and experiences, and you can turn to Chapter 3, 'How to Tailor the Letter to the Job and Company', if you need more help or just a reminder of what to include.

Why you want to work for them

In this paragraph, you highlight to the employer why them, your career aspirations, interest in this type of work and the company. Why are you interested in working for them? Consider your interests and values; what are your career drivers or motivations? You can learn more about career drivers in 'Further Reading and Resources'. This is where your research into the employer is important; you can demonstrate you have spent time researching them as a company. Things that can be included here could range from:

- business values, mission statements;

- their work with local communities, charities and so on;

- awards, that is, Investors in People;

- part of the Stonewall Diversity Champions Programme, or the Disability Confident Scheme.

Suppose you're unsure where to look for this information. In that case, you can start by reviewing the original advert, doing a general search for them online, looking at their website or using social media, for example, LinkedIn, to find out about the company.

Additional information

This paragraph is optional; it can be used for additional information. This could include explaining aspects of your CV, that is, a year out or if you have gaps in your employment history. You can use this paragraph to either explain the context of the gaps or highlight the additional skills and/or transferable skills you gained from this period. You could also consider using this paragraph to share or disclose information, that is, a disability, and request a reasonable adjustment, that is, to be contacted by email or text. If you need more information about sharing or disclosing sensitive information, turn to Chapter 7, 'Disclosing and Sharing Sensitive Information'.

Closing statement

This paragraph is where you end and close your letter. You can thank the employer for considering your application, add details of interview availability, tell them you look forward to hearing from them, that is, in anticipation of your reply and so on. Check that your contact details are correct and the same on your covering letter and CV.

Signing off

Lastly, you need to sign off your letter. If you have included the name of the person you are writing the letter to, you can sign off with 'Yours sincerely'. If you do not and have used a, for example, 'Dear Hiring Manager' sign off with 'Yours faithfully'.

It is also important to include your name in case the two get separated. Consider how you like to be referred to when signing off and adding your name. If you have a long first name then shorten it to, for example, Eva or Olly, or if you use a nickname or a family name, this could add confusion. For further examples of signing off or what is called the salutation, have a look at Chapter 9, 'Digital versus Paper Letters'.

Here is a covering letter template that you can use as a guide when you write your letter.

COMPELLING COVERING LETTERS

Template for a covering letter

Your address
Telephone number
Email address

Name of person, for example, Mr Taylor
Job title
Address

Date.

Dear Mr Taylor

Reference: Job title and/or reference number

First paragraph: Open your letter by '**introducing yourself'**, state you would like to apply for '. . . role', and include where and when you saw the role advertised, for example, 'Indeed' or local paper.

Second paragraph: Highlight '**why you'** briefly note your relevant work experience, including voluntary work and specific skills that link to the job description. Refer to aspects of your CV to link the CV and covering letter together.

Third paragraph: Include '**why them**', your interest in working in the sector, and that company, that is, the reputation and/or values or awards they hold.

Fourth paragraph: This paragraph is optional; it is for **additional information**. You could note additional skills and experiences from a gap year, and so on, and/or share and disclose information such as a disability, that is, request a reasonable adjustment, that is, an alternative form of communication.

Fifth paragraph: This is your **closing statement;** here, you are rounding up your letter, telling the employer you look forward to being called for an interview, noting your availability or holidays, and so on.

Yours sincerely/faithfully

NB: Type your name if you are sending the letter electronically.

The section above outlines the basic ingredients for your covering letter. Your covering letter is personal to you, so you will have individual preferences. Here is a tip on how you can add some personality and demonstrate your enthusiasm in your letter.

A covering letter needs to be in a business letter in a professional format but that does not mean it needs to be neutral and dull. Ideally you want to grab the attention of the reader in the first line showing enthusiasm for the role applied for.

*An example of one that demonstrated motivation and enthusiasm started with 'I was **delighted** to see your advert in The Guardian ref no.' (Kathleen Houston, Career Coach and Senior Teaching Fellow)*

IN A NUTSHELL

- Check the advert for the application requirements, that is, covering letter and/or CV.
- Use the job specification as a checklist.
- Check both your contact details and the employer's are correct.
- Research you and the employer.
- Draft your letter using the basic ingredients: introduce yourself, why you, why them, additional information, close and sign off.
- It's your letter; make it personal to you, not generic.

You can do further research to help you prepare to write your covering letter, as your letter is as important as your CV. Remember to check out 'Further Reading and Resources'.

3 HOW TO TAILOR THE LETTER TO THE JOB AND COMPANY

This chapter covers how to effectively tailor your covering letter to the specific company and job role that you're using it for. This will include researching the employer and highlighting the skills and experience required, as well as the style and content of the letter. It's important to remember that the company and the job are two separate things and should be treated as such. This chapter will show you how to do this.

Part 1 – Tailoring your letter to the job

To enable you to tailor your letter to the job role, you will need a copy of the job description as well as the person specification. You will need to save, download or print a copy of these prior to the application deadline date. Often, once this date has passed, you are no longer able to access this information.

If you are applying speculatively, and therefore do not have a job description or person specification, you can look at the job profiles or job descriptions on websites such as prospects.ac.uk, the National Careers Service or Target Jobs. Each of these will provide you with an overview of what the role entails, the main responsibilities for that role and the key skills needed.

Now carefully read the job description and person specification, highlighting key words and phrases. These would include the skills, experience, qualifications and type of person the employer is looking for. See the 'keywords' section in Chapter 4, 'Words and Language', to learn more about this.

You will have many things that the employer wants, so it's important that the employer knows this. As well as landing you an interview, the purpose of the covering letter, in conjunction with your CV, is to ensure the employer knows that you have what they need. But neither document is very long, so you need to prioritise what you say at this stage. Pick out things that you are good at that the employer has described as essential.

Here is an example of a person specification:

		Assessed in interview (I) or application (A)	Essential (E)	Desirable (D)
Equal opportunities	Awareness of and commitment to equal opportunities	I	E	
Aptitude	Able to work flexibly as part of a team	I, A	E	
	Able to use initiative and prioritise own workload	I		D
	Good communication skills	I, A	E	

		Assessed in interview (I) or application (A)	Essential (E)	Desirable (D)
Skills and abilities	Experience of using ICT such as Word, Excel and PowerPoint	I, A		D
	Able to follow instructions and work to deadlines	I, A	E	
Qualifications	Vocational qualification at level 3 in health and social care	A		D
	GCSEs at grade 4 or above in English, science and maths	A	E	

You'll notice the two columns on the right, which let you know how the employer plans to assess if you've met each of the criteria and whether they deem it to be essential or desirable. Some person specifications are quite short, like the example above, whereas others can be several pages in length. Whichever one is the case for the job you're applying to, when writing your CV and covering letter, you need to focus initially on the criteria which the employer has deemed to be essential and will be assessed through the application. This means that they will be expecting to see these items referred to either in your CV, covering letter or personal statement, and if they aren't, this could have a negative impact on you receiving an interview invitation.

By ensuring that you have addressed some of the employer's criteria and requirements, you will boost your chances of being offered an interview. It also demonstrates to the employer that you have read the details of the job and know what it is you are applying to do. Most employers will very clearly see the difference between an applicant who has read the job details and tailored their application accordingly and one that has copied and pasted or just submitted a generic application.

Here are some examples you can adapt and use:

1. As a careers prefect, alongside others, I was tasked with meeting and greeting visiting employers during a mock interview day at school. I was praised for my politeness and efficiency by several employers.
2. As a trainee editor, it was imperative that I follow the brief accurately and meet the deadline. I was proud of achieving this for all articles.

Part 2 –Tailoring your letter to the employer

Everyone likes to be made to feel special, and an employer is no different. When you're writing your covering letter, you need to try to make them feel like they are the only company you are applying to, and you only want to work for them. You can achieve this by doing a bit of research about the company before starting to write your letter.

Use the following places to find out more about the company or organisation:

● The company website.

● The companies' pages on social media sites such as LinkedIn, Facebook, Instagram and X.

● Any information the company may have sent you when you enquired about the role.

- People who have previously or currently worked there asking, for company insights.

- Websites which include company reviews and ratings such as Glassdoor and Indeed.

The type of information you're looking for could include the company's values, ethos, benefits package, location, work ethic, staff groups and what they're like to work for.

While researching the company, ask yourself questions about what is important to you and why that company and role jumped out at you. Possible questions could be:

- Do they have a creche or family-friendly childcare policy?

- Do they have a reputation for treating their employees well?

- Do they offer their employees opportunities for progression or training?

- Have people you've spoken with talked about the company in a positive way?

- Do they have active staff networks, including ethnic minority, women's, LGBT+ or disability?

- Do their values align with yours? For example, are their products sustainable, do they value continuous learning, is it a fun place to work and so on?

- Are they located somewhere that you can easily get to?

If it seems that the company can deliver what you believe is important, remember to mention this in your covering letter. But don't make a huge list; prioritise the top two or three. Remember, you need to hold a bit back, so you have something to say in the interview.

Here are three examples:

1. I am excited at the prospect of working for a company that puts its staff before profits, values the impact of continuous professional development and looks like a fun place to work.
2. Working for a forward-thinking company such as yours, which has world-class facilities alongside international work opportunities, is something I aspire to.
3. As a member of the LGBTQ+ community, I was pleased to see that you sponsored the local pride march last year and have an active LGBTQ+ staff network. These things, alongside your inspirational company values, are what have drawn me to apply to work for you.

Style and content

With every applicant vying for the employer's attention, it's the little things that are going to potentially make a big difference.

Consider the following questions:

- On the employer's website or literature, do they use a particular style of writing? Is it formal, professional, technical, informal, humorous and so on?

- Do particular phrases get mentioned more than once in the company's information?

- Is there a font or colour scheme used repeatedly by the employer?

- Considering what the company does, who are their services aimed at? Is it children, the elderly, international clients, the general public, industry professionals?

Have the answers to these questions in mind when writing your covering letter and adapt it accordingly. For example, if the company is offering a service aimed at younger people and many of its employees are under the age of 30, you don't want your letter to come across as too formal or old fashioned. Alternatively, if you are applying to a governing body within a specific vocational area, then your letter needs to come across as formal and professional.

Most covering letters will either be printed in black ink on a white page or be attached as such to an email. If you are applying to a creative role you may want to present your letter and accompanying CV in a more creative way. One simple way of doing this is by using the same font style and colour as the employer does in the literature or on their website.

There is a saying which some people may be familiar with which is 'show don't tell'. If you can show something rather than having to write it, it can be an effective way of keeping your letter concise. For example, if the employer is asking for someone who pays close attention to detail, by ensuring that everything in your letter is spelt correctly, is grammatically correct, the layout is consistent throughout and you have mentioned everything they've asked for, you've shown this without having to tell it. This is also an excellent way for creative people to show their skills. Rather than writing 'I am a very creative individual with excellent graphic design skills'. Consider using graphic design elements within your CV and covering letter which show this instead. With every sentence in your covering letter, ask yourself, is there a way I can show this so that I don't need to tell it? You can learn more about the style of your cover letter in Chapter 10, 'Style and Substance'.

By paying attention to these small things and using some of them within your covering letter, it lets the employer know several things. First, that you have done your research on them. Secondly, that you have put some time and effort into this application which demonstrates that you're keen, and hopefully reflects that you'll put the same amount of time and effort into the job if you get it. Finally, it shows that this isn't a copied and pasted letter that you've used before, it's a letter tailored specifically for them.

IN A NUTSHELL

- Read the job description (JD) and person specification (PS) carefully.
- Research the role as well as the employer.
- Pick out key points from the JD and PS and mention these in your letter.
- Attempt to show not tell where possible.

4 WORDS AND LANGUAGE

If you want your covering letter to catch the attention of the person reading it, which you do, you need to make effective use of compelling and persuasive language.

Your letter needs to convince the recruiter that you have what they want and that it's worth inviting you to the next stage of the recruitment process. This isn't going to happen if your letter sends them to sleep!

Understanding the purpose of your letter

To enable you to write your letter effectively, you need to understand its purpose. This may seem obvious: you want a job, so that's the purpose of the letter. But that's not the primary purpose of your covering letter. Your letter serves two main purposes. The first is to introduce you to the employer, and the second is to persuade the employer to invite you in for an interview. Once you know this, you should find it a bit easier to write your letter.

The power to persuade

Do not confuse being persuasive with begging.

According to the *Cambridge Dictionary* – persuade means:

> to make someone do or believe something by giving them a good reason to do it or by talking to that person and making them believe it.

Whereas as beg means:

> to make a very strong and urgent request.

The difference being that persuading is a well-composed written or verbal means of making someone do something that you want. In this case that would be to invite you in for an interview and ultimately, give you a job. Begging, on the other hand, is simply asking for something without providing any good cause or reason for the person to say yes. So, as this distinction hopefully shows, you are not begging for the job; you are showing the employer that you are the best person for the job through highlighting your relevant skills, experiences and strengths.

A simple technique, often used by speechwriters, is the rule of three. People are used to hearing things in threes such as 'reduce, reuse, recycle' or you may know that the triangle with its three sides is one of the strongest shapes. Therefore, using the rule of three in your letter can be very powerful. Did you notice this technique was used in the previous paragraph with the mention of skills, experiences and strengths? The rule of three not only refers to the words you use but the topics covered too. Ideally, sticking to three key pieces of information is enough. For example, (1) introduction to you and why you are writing to them, (2) why you'd be the best person for the job and (3) why you want to work for them. If you overload your letter with too much information, the recruiter will not be able to retain it all. Therefore, prioritise three key things and keep it at that.

If you remind yourself of your English language lessons in school, you'll notice that the words 'reduce', 'reuse' and 'recycle' are all verbs. Verbs are excellent to use as persuasive tools as opposed to adjectives which are purely descriptive.

Power words

The use of, what are often referred to as, power words or action verbs is important within your letter. Action verbs are dynamic in nature and let the recruiter know the extent of your involvement and responsibility regarding the skill or role you are describing. For example, rather than saying that you *know how to write reports* you could say that you have *conducted research and generated reports.* The first example uses a passive verb and leaves the recruiter wondering whether you've written any reports yourself whereas the second uses two action verbs and the recruiter has a clearer picture of what you've done. Importantly, the same number of words has been used. It doesn't take extra words to tell the employer more. See the section about being concise later in this chapter.

Here's a list of 50 power words to get you started.

Achieved	Demonstrated	Headed	Pioneered
Administered	Developed	Handled	Project-managed
Analysed	Devised	Implemented	Promoted
Arranged	Directed	Improved	Represented
Assessed	Eliminated	Initiated	Researched
Built	Encouraged	Introduced	Responsible
Chaired	Evaluated	Launched	Rewarded for
Collaborated	Executed	Led	Spearheaded
Collated	Expanded	Liaised	Succeeded in
Conceptualised	Formalised	Managed	Suggested
Conducted	Formulated	Oversaw	Supervised
Coordinated	Founded	Organised	
Created	Generated	Planned	

Keywords

As well as power verbs, it's also important to use keywords within your covering letter. Keywords refer to the employers' priorities, and they will be looking for candidates that meet them. You can usually work out what these are when reading a job description or person specification. You will already have read about doing this in Chapter 3, 'How to Tailor the Letter to the Job and Company'. In the excerpt from a job description below, all the keywords have been underlined:

- Used to receiving <u>feedback</u> with a <u>positive, can-do attitude</u>.

- Excellent <u>communication skills</u> and an ability to <u>build strong working relationships</u>.

- A <u>flexible, proactive</u> approach to tasks and a natural <u>collaborator</u>.

Your job, within the covering letter as well as your accompanying CV, is to ensure each of the underlined words is mentioned once. You do not need to repeat each one several times to emphasise that you have it; mentioning it once is enough. If the job description or person specification is long, pick out the keywords within the areas that the employer has marked as essential rather than desirable, or focus on what you feel their priorities are or your top strengths. Remember that the covering letter and CV work in collaboration. Don't feel that you must cram everything into your covering letter; save some for your CV and vice versa.

Some employers use applicant tracking systems (ATS) to help them sort through high volumes of applications. Usually, these systems have been programmed with certain keywords that they search for within CVs and covering letters. Therefore, when writing your covering letter, try to use the same wording the employer does in the job description or person specification, as this is likely to match what the ATS has been programmed to find. You can read more about ATS in the next chapter.

Be concise

It's important to add that the letter needs to be concise and avoid unnecessary waffle. This means that you need to find a way of saying a lot by using as few words as possible. Every word needs to have a reason for being there. Making use of verbs rather than adjectives is one way to help you write more concisely. Verbs get to the point quicker, whereas adjectives can sometimes be viewed as optional extras that can be omitted without losing any of the sentences meaning.

For example,

'During my time at ABC Ltd, whilst working as a laboratory technician, for part of my role I was responsible for overseeing a wide range of things, which included the safe handling of toxic materials and making sure all necessary procedures and safety guidelines were adhered to by everyone involved'.

could become:

'At ABC Ltd, I was responsible for ensuring the safe handling of toxic materials and that safety protocols were adhered to.'

The second example conveys the same information but uses 20 words rather than 50. There are three verbs within the sentence and just one adjective (verbs — responsible, ensure and adhere; adjective — safe).

Having removed the section 'for part of my role I was responsible for overseeing a wide range of things' won't harm your chances. Read this part to yourself and picture what it's telling the employer. You'll hopefully realise that it isn't telling them much and can therefore be deleted from your letter.

Taking out the specific job role here isn't a problem as this will be listed in your CV within the employment section.

Being concise can sometimes be challenging and takes practice. You may find it easier to start by writing your letter without worrying about which words you use or how many. Once you're happy that you've covered everything, edit the letter by changing each passive verb to an action verb. Once you've done this, reread each sentence and think of alternative ways you can say the same thing using fewer words and removing unnecessary adjectives. It may take several rewrites to get it right, but it's worth spending the time to do this as it increases your chances of getting through to the next stage of the application process.

Using generative AI (GenAI)

You may be tempted to use GenAI such as ChatGPT to help you write your covering letter. This will provide you with a basic letter to get you started, but it's essential that you edit this using your own words and language to ensure it is authentic and reflects your personality. By entering the keywords from the job description into a GenAI system, a standard letter will be produced, but it's likely the employer will receive numerous identical letters from other candidates. To make sure you stand out from the crowd, your letter needs to look and sound different from everyone else's. The best way to do this is to write it yourself using words that you use rather than those suggested by GenAI. Read more about AI in Chapter 5, 'The Use of AI and Covering Letters'.

IN A NUTSHELL

- Be persuasive without begging.
- Use the rule of three.
- Use power verbs rather than passive verbs and adjectives.
- Read the job description and insert keywords from this into your letter.
- Be concise and don't repeat yourself.
- Be authentic and don't rely on GenAI to write your letter for you.

5 THE USE OF AI WITH COVERING LETTERS

We are living in an age where we are surrounded by artificial intelligence (AI). Examples of AI that many of us take for granted include Amazon's Alexa, Apple's Siri, Google Maps and the sat-navs in many of our cars. The type of AI that could help in covering letter writing is called a chatbot. The original and best-known chatbot is ChatGPT, but there are other versions out there, including Microsoft Copilot, Meta's Llama, Gemini and Bard. These are all generative AI, which is a form of AI that analyses huge amounts of data, images and text from multiple sources to produce a new and original answer to prompts it has received. Prompts are the instructions or queries that you input to elicit a response, and in this case, the response would be a covering letter.

Another form of AI that you will possibly encounter during the job application process, often unknowingly, is an applicant tracking system (ATS). These are AI-driven software packages which help make the job of sifting through large numbers of job applications more efficient and less labour-intensive. When you are asked to submit your CV and covering letter online, it is likely that initially, it is being uploaded to an ATS. Unfortunately, this also means that if you are not successful, it could be the ATS communicating with you about this rather than a human. As technology evolves, it is being asked to undertake more and more complex tasks, and assisting in the recruitment process is one of these.

This chapter will help you:

- use generative AI to write a covering letter;

- be aware of the pros and cons of using AI in covering letter writing;

- recognise applicant tracking systems;

- know how to produce a letter that applicant tracking system software will be able to read.

Four steps to producing a covering letter using AI

It is very possible to write a covering letter using AI alone, and this will speed up your application process quite a lot, but this is not recommended because it won't be your words the employer will be reading; it will be the AI's. The best option, if you wish to use AI, is to work in collaboration with it, and here's how.

1. Sign in to your chosen chatbot and write the first prompt, for example:

   'Please write a covering letter for the role of nursery nurse at Little Lambs Nursery. Here is a copy of the job description.'

This will produce a covering letter, but not one that is about you. It won't have any mention of you or what you can offer the employer. It will, though, make assumptions so check these carefully. In an interview, you could be asked about any of the information you've provided within your CV and covering letter. You don't want to get caught out because the AI has said you did something which you didn't.

2. Add another prompt asking for more personal information to be added and be specific about what you want.

> 'Edit the letter to include my three key skills which are communication, creativity and record keeping. Mention that I have had 2 years' work experience in childcare too.'

This will result in a letter that is more focussed on your experience and skills. If you would like the letter to include more information from your CV, you could provide a copy of your CV to the chatbot and ask it to incorporate these details into the letter too.

3. Read the resulting letter and continue adding prompts until you are happy with the result.
4. Take the AI-produced letter and inject a bit of your personality and authenticity into it by using the advice in the rest of this book.

Keep in mind, the resulting letter is only as good as the prompts you write and the information you provide, as it is these that the chatbot is using to enable it to write an effective letter. The more time and effort you put into it, the better the final covering letter will be.

Adding authenticity

Unless you tell it, the AI won't know what words you typically do and don't use, which is where your careful editing is required. The letter shouldn't read like a thesaurus of great words that the AI has included, especially if these are words that you don't typically use and may not even know what they mean. Similarly, the sentences should be structured in a manner that is reflective of how you normally express yourself when in a formal situation. Again, the AI can attempt to replicate this if you provide it with enough prompts, but your editing will provide more authenticity. Some AIs have been known to create quite elaborate language which few people speak like ordinarily. Chapter 4 talks more about words and language and includes the use of AI.

Be aware

ChatGPT is owned by OpenAI, which, like many other AI developers, is an American organisation. This is important to remember as some of the words within the letter it produces may have American spellings such as 'program' instead of 'programme' and 'advisor' instead of 'adviser'. It may also use American terminology such as 'resumé' instead of 'CV'. Unless you are aware and keeping your eyes open for this type of thing, they would be easy to miss, but to an employer, they could be a tell-tale sign that you have used AI to help you write your letter.

Stating a desired length for the letter will let the AI know how long or short you want it to be. The danger is, once you have read the awesome, but long, letter the AI has devised for you, it'll be hard to know what to remove. So, remember to include in your prompts a paragraph or approximate word count to enable the AI to write to this limit.

Chat versus Bot

It's useful to remember the word 'chat' within chatbot. It should feel like you are having a conversation with the chatbot. You can ask it to tweak sentences to emphasise specific points, to change words to something you'd prefer, as well as amend the overall letter to make it more or less formal.

The flip side of this, though, is the word 'bot' within chatbot. One of the dangers of using a chatbot to write a letter for you is that it will read very much like a robot has written it because essentially, that's what a chatbot is. An employer isn't looking to employ a robot; they are looking for a person with a personality, and it is essential that you attempt to portray some of this in your letter. Again, this is where your editing can make all the difference and turn a standard AI-written letter into something that accurately represents you as a person.

What do employers think?

There will undoubtedly be employers who are either unconcerned or unaware of how many applicants for jobs with them have used AI to help write their covering letters. But on the flip side, there are some employers who are very concerned and are taking steps to combat the use of AI. Some companies have banned or limited their employees from using AI in the workplace, so you can be confident that these companies are not going to look favourably upon an applicant who has used AI to apply for a position with them. If you are planning to use AI when applying, make sure you do your research on the company to check if they have publicised their views on the use of AI. Many employers will have policies in place advising how and for what purposes their employees are permitted to use AI in the workplace. Some companies have gone as far as purchasing AI detection software such as GPTZero to flag any AI-generated content.

The quotes overleaf are from people involved in the shortlisting and recruitment process in a large secondary school.

If I received an AI cover letter, I doubt I would spot it during the shortlisting process, and it may well secure them an interview.

However, if on interview the candidate didn't seem to match the person that they had presented on paper this would make me suspicious and doubt their integrity. Therefore, they would be less likely to be successful at interview. (Sarah Lewis, Head of School)

I would have concerns with the application or cover letter if it was clearly written by AI. I think that a key aspect of the covering letter is demonstrating the skill of writing and communicating effectively with an audience in mind. If that is done by AI, I would be concerned that the applicant either doesn't have those skills, is not confident in those skills, or has not put much time into the application – and by extension would question how much do they want this job. For many roles, writing ability might not be important and therefore would not be as much of a concern. Equally, it would require me to know it is AI, which would be trickier now, especially if the applicant has spent some time reading the AI output and amending where required. (Stuart Ward, Deputy Head Teacher)

As you can see from these two quotes from employers, they may not always spot that AI has been used initially, but they will become suspicious if there is an obvious disconnect between the style and standard of the application in comparison to the individual that arrives for an interview. In addition, if you have asked the AI to state that you have excellent written communication skills, yet you are relying on an AI to do this for you, if discovered by the employer, they may decide not to offer you the job. They may worry that if you have used an AI to write your application, which elements of the job with them would you also be planning to use AI for? As one employer implies, for some roles, writing ability is less important than in others, so think very carefully about the job you are applying for and what it involves before deciding whether using AI to help you apply for it is a good idea.

Can AI recognise AI?

It is fairly common practice for employers, especially larger ones, to make use of AI themselves within the recruitment process, as it can be useful in helping them sift through large numbers of applications quickly. The systems they use are called applicant tracking systems (ATS).

There are four main steps in which the ATS plays a pivotal role.

Step 1 – The employer will submit the details of the job into the ATS, specifying the job title, key skills needed, required qualifications and desired amount of experience.

Step 2 – Using the information provided, the ATS creates a profile of the ideal applicant.

Step 3 – Upon receipt of your covering letter and CV, it will scan and critically analyse these documents and conduct a virtual box-ticking exercise.

Step 4 – If your letter and CV have ticked the right number of boxes, you will progress to the next stage of the application process.

Unfortunately, not every file type or format of document can be read by some ATS. Many ATS aren't designed to understand documents that have lots of formatting within them, which some AI-generated documents contain. If you do use an AI-produced letter, ensure that you remove all unnecessary formatting prior to clicking submit.

Applicant tracking systems are not programmed to spot AI-generated letters; they are simply an efficiency tool for shortlisting candidates. But the next step in the process will most likely be a human reviewing the top applications. Prompting the

AI to load your letter with keywords from the job description and using elaborate language may impress an ATS, but it is unlikely to please the human in HR who will read your letter next. The purpose of a covering letter is to convince an employer that you have the required skills, experience and qualifications to do the job they've advertised. If using AI isn't going to help you achieve this goal, then don't use it.

Over to you

Whether or not you choose to make use of AI to help you write your covering letter is a personal choice, but what is clear is that it still takes time and effort to do it properly. You will need to use carefully worded prompts, provide the AI with relevant documentation to inform it of what you want included as well as excluded, and you will need to ensure it isn't using words and language that you don't understand or wouldn't normally use. Use AI as a tool, not the solution.

IN A NUTSHELL

- Use AI in collaboration with your own words and edits, not as a stand-alone tool.
- Most AI companies are American, so amend to ask it to use UK English.
- Carefully check any assumptions the AI has made and remove or edit as necessary.
- The better the prompts and information you provide the AI, the better the resulting output will be.
- Remove formatting to ensure it can be read by applicant tracking systems.

6 ONE SIZE DOESN'T ALWAYS FIT ALL

Throughout this book, it has been reiterated that 'one size doesn't always fit all', and hopefully reminded you that if you want your covering letter to be successful, it can't be generic; it needs to be researched and tailored. The content of your letter will change depending on where you are in your career journey, for example, you're a graduate, student, a job changer or a first-time job seeker.

As one size doesn't fit all, this chapter will cover:

- part-time job applicants/first-time job seekers;

- graduates job changers;

- job changers;

- EU and/or international applicants.

While this chapter aims to cover the different types of covering letters, sometimes there is an overlap in these various stages of your career, for example, you can be a graduate applying for a part-time job and be a first-time job seeker. Therefore, while each section describes specific elements that should be included or omitted in this type of letter and will give you some examples of what to include, there is some overlap.

This chapter will help you:

- tailor your covering letter whether you're a first-time applicant or a graduate;

- consider your unique selling points (USP) when one size doesn't fit all;

- raise your awareness of what employers will be looking for.

Part-time applicants/first-time job seekers

You may be considering applying for a part-time job, and this might be to fit alongside your studies. It may not directly relate to your career aspirations but is more about earning income and building transferable skills. This could be your first job as you may not have been employed before. If it is your first application, you will more likely have limited experience to draw from and to refer to when writing your CV and covering letter. If this is the case, it is essential that you spend some time analysing your transferable skills. Now, you may not have heard of this term before. So, what does it mean?

A **transferable skill** is any skill that you have and can be used in various situations.

There are several tools that you can access to help you gain a better understanding of your transferable skills. Wherever you are studying, they may have their own resources to help you assess your skills. If you are at a college or university, your career leader or team is an ideal port of call for this type of help. Reach out to them, have an appointment and find out what resources they have in their career areas. They may also signpost you to external resources, that is:

- www.prospects.ac.uk
- www.myworldofwork.co.uk
- www.nationalcareers.service.gov.uk

All these resources have tools to help you better understand your transferable skills and will probably have a skills assessment tool. You can use these or create your own skills audit tool, which you can save on your computer. Use the QR code or URL at the start of this book and download the 'Employability skills audit tool' and 'Skills dictionary' or go to the 'Transferable skills in more detail' section later in this chapter, if you download the documents, then you can save and personalise them for your own use.

You may not be familiar with or understand all the terminology used in these types of skills audits. However, it is better to realise, sooner rather than later, that you are unsure of the terminology, rather than being in an interview situation and unable to provide evidence of this, just because you are not exactly sure what they are asking for evidence of.

In my experience, many students struggle with terms like 'interpersonal'. When I delivered workshops on transferable skills, this was often the one that students didn't quite get or understand.

Below is an explanation of the term 'interpersonal':

Interpersonal: the ability to relate to and feel comfortable with people at all levels and to be able to make and maintain relationships as circumstances change. Listener, adviser, counsellor, politically aware, initiator, cooperative, constructive, assertive.

It is essential to fully understand the terminology used in applications and the recruitment process. Without knowing what is being asked for, how can you possibly give an example of your experiences or say you have 'excellent interpersonal skills, developed through your time as . . .'?

The basic ingredients for your part-time or first-time job seeker covering letter remain similar to those in Chapter 2, 'Understanding What Should Be in Each Section'. If you are a part-time applicant or first-time job seeker and you have limited experience to draw on, then in paragraph two, you need to highlight your transferable skills.

EXAMPLE FOR PART-TIME WORK

First paragraph: Start with your introduction and why you are writing, 'I would like to apply for a part-time role at xxxxxx.' Include where and when you saw the role advertised.

Second paragraph: Highlight **'why you'**. If you have any experience from clubs, volunteering and/or studies, you can add this here. Here, it's important to outline your transferable skills, for example, I have excellent communication and leadership skills from my studies, group projects and presentations.

Undergraduate or graduate

If you are at the end of your studies or just graduated, depending on what type of role you are applying for, consider focusing on different aspects of your skills and experience. You might wonder what I mean when I say this! If you are applying for part-time work in retail or hospitality, which is more about keeping some earnings coming in. When you write a letter for this type of application, in all honesty, this employer will be less interested in the fact that you are a graduate and more interested in your skills and experiences. Sometimes, students find this hard to grasp, but this employer wants someone to start working in their business, and they might be less concerned about your graduate aspirations. In this case, consider what you include in your covering letter when writing your letter. If you have limited experience, you will have gained and developed a range of transferable skills that you can draw on in this part of your letter and CV. Look at the section above, which outlines what transferable skills are and how to audit your skill set. So, when applying for a part-time job, consider the employer, what they want and what skills you can offer them.

In the example below, the main changes in this letter are in the second paragraph.

EXAMPLE FOR PART-TIME WORK

First paragraph: Start with your introduction and explain why you are writing 'I would like to apply for' . . . role. Include where and when you saw the role advertised.

Second paragraph: Highlight **'why you'** and highlight your relevant work experience, as well as your specific skills and transferable skills, rather than your degree and graduate studies.

If you're applying for a role relevant to your graduate studies or where there might be a graduate programme or an employer looking for graduate-level education, consider highlighting your graduate qualifications at the outset of your letter. In paragraph two, highlight any related work experience, your transferable skills, live projects key modules and so on.

EXAMPLE FOR A GRADUATE COVERING LETTER

First paragraph: Start with your introduction and why you are writing, such as 'I am a third-year **graduate** or I have a degree in Computer design and am on track to achieve a 2;1' and 'I would like to apply for . . . role' and include where and when you saw the role advertised.

Second paragraph: Highlight **'why you'** and your relevant work experience, your specific skills and transferable skills, and your degree studies, such as specific modules, for example, C++, 3D graphics or name live projects with specific companies.

It could also be the case that this application is your first job seeker application, and as such, as outlined above, it is vital that you assess your skills. Refer to the section above on how first-time job seekers get to grips with the terminology around transferable skills, as you might not realise you already have a wealth of these skills, for example, teamwork and communication skills. If you have been working and studying or worked in hospitality or retail in a shop or bar, you also have additional transferable skills. Often, it's easy to overlook these skills, but as a bartender, you will have gained and developed your negotiation, communication, teamwork skills and so on. So, whether your covering letter is for your first job, or your first graduate job, spend time auditing your skills, and the main changes to your covering letter will be as outlined above.

Job changers

You might be happy in your current job. However, while past generations may have stayed in their jobs for many years, the reality is that in your lifetime, you are likely to have, on average, in the region of 12 jobs and stay with an employer for, on average, just over four years (Zippia, 2023). In the latter half of 2023, approximately 2.9% of people in the United Kingdom moved to a new job (Statista, 2023). In fact, since the Covid-19 pandemic, people have felt less satisfied with their work-life balance, and many more want something different from their career journey, not only the role they undertake but also the work-life balance. In 2022, ACAS noted that three in five employers (60%) have seen an increase in hybrid working, such as working flexibly split between the workplace and working from home or remotely. This trend is likely to remain, and a recent report by Prospects (2023) says that '96% of graduates said that working/life balance was fairly or very important to them when looking for a job'.

It could be that you have had a career in one sector, you are looking for more flexible working, or you have a change of direction. For example, you could have returned to education to be a nurse or a social worker, or you have decided to formalise your experience and gain qualifications to support a job change, for example, business and marketing studies.

No matter the reason for your job change, it is essential to spend some time and consider which aspects of your skills and experiences are most sellable to a new employer. If it is in a similar sector, then that is easier. You can cross-sell your current skills and experiences, use your current job specification to remind you of your duties, skills, and experiences that your current employer required, and use these when writing your letter. However, suppose you are moving to a job in a different sector. In that case, you do need to spend time understanding your transferable skills, researching what the new sector will require, and benchmarking yourself against any new job specification. This is important if you have been in your current post for some time, as it is easy to undervalue and sell your skills. Use the section above to remind yourself what transferable skills you have and do a new audit (use the activity above). This new insight will be invaluable when writing your CV and covering letter.

The basic ingredients for your covering letter remain similar. Again, you will need to introduce yourself in the first paragraph, and then in the second paragraph, highlight why you are the best applicant. If it's a similar sector, you can sell your years of experience. However, if you are applying to a different sector, consider which bits of your skills and experiences are more sellable.

Below are two examples, the first if you are staying in the same sector and the second if you are moving to a different sector:

EXAMPLE FOR JOB CHANGER COVERING LETTER – SAME SECTOR

First paragraph: Start with your introduction, and why you are writing 'I am an experienced computer designer, with ten years' experience in a commercial setting . . .'

Second paragraph: Highlight **'why you',** highlighting your directly relevant work experience, specific skills and transferable skills, including industry-related qualifications and training, for example, C++ and JarvaScript (JS).

EXAMPLE FOR JOB CHANGER COVERING LETTER – DIFFERENT SECTOR

First paragraph: Start with your introduction and why you are writing '. . . I was pleased to see your recent advert and call for applications for a new Computer designer'.

Second paragraph: Highlight **'why you'** and highlight your relevant or related work experience. For example, as part of your computer design role, you dealt directly with customers; therefore, you have ten years of direct customer service experience in a commercial setting. Outline your transferable skills, for example, customer service, communication and negotiation skills.

As with your CV, it is essential to consider what to include in your covering letter, particularly if you are a job changer. It is easy to fall back on what you know, but it is important to consider what the new employer will be looking for, so you may have to rely on your transferable skills.

European and/or international applicants

If you are a European (EU) and/or international student, you might be used to a very different format when writing a CV and covering letter. Your home country may have different preferences when it comes to content, for example, in some countries, CVs include a photograph, which is not included on a UK CV. It is best to connect to your career leader or team at the institution you are studying; they will have resources on how to write a covering letter and what type of content is expected. If you are currently studying in the UK and applying for a post here too, there are several things I would suggest you consider:

Qualifications

If the bulk of your qualifications had been achieved in another country, then spend some time ascertaining what these qualifications are equivalent to. It may be challenging to get exact equivalencies. You could try the following to help you gauge what they might be:

- Universities usually give guidance on entry requirements for EU and international students:

    If you are from Poland and completed your general secondary education, studying English, maths, biology and so on, and received your maturity certificate or Matura, some institutions accept this as an equivalent to both A Levels and GCSE.

    Manchester University states the entry requirements for an undergraduate course is:

    'Matura/Swiadectwo Dojrzalosci (Secondary School Certificate) qualification with at least three subjects at extended level.'

    If you are from Bangladesh, you may have completed your higher secondary certificate; however, to apply for an undergraduate degree, you would also need either A levels or an international baccalaureate to apply.

    Some universities, such as Warwick, provide a full list of a wide variety of EU and international entry requirements, which can give you some idea of how your qualifications match GCSEs and A levels.

- If you require a more formal acknowledgement of your qualifications and their equivalent, you can contact UK ENIC, the UK National Information Centre. The cost is £49.50 + VAT, but your application can include a maximum of six qualifications.

You can refer to Chapter 2, 'Understanding What Should Be in Each Section', to help better set out your covering letter and to consider what to include in each paragraph. As an EU or international applicant, consider what other selling points you may have. Many employers over recent years have acknowledged the value of recruiting individuals who have a 'Global Mindset' or are seen as 'Global Graduates'. The Global Graduates into Global Leaders (2011) state for an individual to be seen as a global graduate, they need to possess a range of knowledge and key attributes such as some we are used to hearing, for example, teamwork, flexibility and so on and others less known, for example, 'Global Acumen' or 'Cultural Agility'. Global employers such as Pricewaterhouse Cooper and AVIVA have acknowledged that their business is trading in a changing world, working across different cultures, and they need to employ individuals from various countries and cultures. They highlighted that they, as a company, need global agility.

Now, you might not have heard these terms before, so below is a brief explanation.

Global Acumen: the ability to work with different people, consider situations from various perspectives and have cross-border collaboration skills and intercultural awareness.

Global Agility: a function that enables the organisation to manage its global workforce supply/demand equation.

When you write your covering letter, as an EU or international student, you will be more likely to be aware of different cultures from your lived experience in your own country, and your host country will be studying in the UK. You can draw on these experiences in your CV and covering letter and highlight why you and what you have to offer that someone who hasn't had these experiences can. You might not be sure exactly what is classed as work experience, the quote below reminds you what it is and what can be included.

> *Work experience comes in all shapes and forms and there are many different contexts (paid, unpaid, formal, informal) where you can develop the skills employers are looking for. Firstly, include experiences from your home country. Don't discount roles outside the UK; this can be your unique selling point, showcasing cultural awareness and international business insights.*
>
> *Secondly, don't underestimate the benefits of experiences outside your immediate sector of interest – you may see opportunities that on the surface don't seem relevant, but these can provide you with a range of transferable skills to help you with your next steps. (Monira Ahmed, Careers Consultant (arts and law))*

English as a second language

Chapter 4, 'Words and Language', covers how to make your letter persuasive; it includes 50 power words and outlines keywords and phrases. If English is not your first language, you may struggle to find the appropriate words when writing your letter. It could be that you are trying to impress the employer and, in so doing, use flowery or over-exaggerated words. As such, the employer can be left feeling that they are not appropriate for the context. Many years ago, I saw an example of this in a student's CV; in their personal statement, they had used a word which meant 'on fire'; the word was not appropriate or in the proper context for the CV. You may want to consider including your additional language skills in your letter and/or CV if you consider these additional selling points. If English is your second language, seek further help and support. If you are at a school, college or university, ask if the careers team can offer feedback on your covering letter. If you are at a university, they will probably have a team that provides support with academic skills, and they will usually read through CVs and covering letters. In addition, you can use the 'spelling and grammar' functions on your Microsoft Word software and ask a friend or family member to read through the letter for you.

Transferable skills in more detail

The Future Demand for Skills in 2030 (2017) report notes the skills that will be in greater demand, such as interpersonal skills and the importance of social skills. Skills development is continually a topic of debate, which skills are seen as most needed and can change. A recent report by the National Foundation for Education Research (NFER) highlighted the top 20 skills, which are unlikely to change due to their transferable nature, for example, communicating with others, including supervisors and peers, and maintaining interpersonal relationships.

In the section below, I have defined several skills that are included in the 'Employability skills audit tool' and provided some examples of where you may have used these skills.

Skills dictionary:

Teamwork is the ability to work well with others in your team or wider team. While working with others, you are flexible; you can adapt to the demands of your workplace and team. Words that can be used to describe you in this situation include communicator, delegator, facilitator, supportive, open-minded and so on.

Example: As a customer service assistant, you will be working as part of a team, whether small or large.

You may, as a team member, work with others in your team to stock the shop floor for a new promotion or seasonal product, such as Christmas. Each of you has a specific area to fill; together with your team members, you discuss who will cover a specific part of the store, and you coordinate with each other, ensuring the new promotion is in place for the Christmas deadline in line with the store marketing. Or, as a team member, you have a rota to ensure there are enough staff to meet the demands of the business. A team member is off sick, and you arrange a meeting with your colleagues and discuss how you can cover their absence, you negotiate with each other who can work when to ensure there are enough staff to meet customer demands.

If you have not had any work experience, you will no doubt still have experience of teamwork from your studies, as outlined in the example in the interpersonal section. You may also be part of a club or sport; these are also great sources of evidence, for examples of teamwork.

Example: You are a member of a football club or netball team.

You are an active member of the team, and as such, you work with your other teammates. You meet regularly to train and discuss team performance. You help motivate other team members, and during the season, you help to arrange travel to matches and events to raise funds to support the team.

In this example, you are a team member and playing as a team, your teamwork skills can be drawn from this as well as the support you give to others, how you meet as a team and discuss strategies going forward to improve team performance and so on.

Leadership: You can, when needed, take control of a situation or lead the team, you can motivate and support others. You can have a wider view of the situation and work needed. When you take on a leadership role, you will also be using a host of other skills, such as communication, problem-solving and decision-making. The words you can use to describe yourself in this situation are motivator, forward/outward-looking, influence, guidance and initiative.

Example: You may think you haven't had leadership experience or managed a team; however, this experience can be gained through a range of different situations, including those that are non-managerial. Earlier, we looked at the example of teamwork. If you were the person who took the lead in either the work situation or sorting out the issues for your university presentation, you'll also have examples of your leadership skills.

> *As a team member, you may work with others in your team to stock the shop floor for a new promotion for Christmas. While each of you has your area to fill, the team can't agree on how to manage the restock for the whole floor and who should do what. You have experience from previous promotions, and you outline to the rest of your colleagues the successful approaches of earlier years; you inform them of the timescales and commitment needed and suggest which colleague should do which area, drawing on your knowledge of their skills and expertise. Some of the newer colleagues need further guidance and motivation to help them complete the tasks at hand. Your leadership input helps the team complete the tasks, and your team is commended by the floor manager for your performance and effective use of staff time.*

If you don't have work experience, don't worry; you can still find examples from other non-managerial situations where you have demonstrated leadership skills. In the section above, I outlined an example of teamwork, such as from school, college or university studies.

As part of the group project, often one member of the team needs to be assertive and take the lead. Was this you? You may have realised that the group was struggling and took the responsibility to create an action plan/work schedule from which the team could then work. You may have delegated, using your knowledge of the group, to identify which members of the group would be better suited to specific tasks, for example, one peer may have great tech skills and could create the visuals for the presentation, while another was best at researching and finding information. Taking the lead in this situation probably helped the team feel better about their workload, and as an outcome, the group presentation received good feedback, and you passed your assignment.

Interpersonal: the ability to relate to and feel comfortable with people at all levels and to be able to make and maintain relationships as circumstances change. You can describe yourself as a listener, adviser, counsellor, politically aware, initiator, cooperative, constructive and assertive.

Spend some time thinking about where and when you have used this skill set. Think about a situation when you actively listened to someone, such as in a work situation.

Example: You are working as a customer service assistant in a retail setting.

A customer has complained about the service they have received or brought a product back and might be frustrated. You spend time listening to the customer, being patient and allowing them the time to express their complaint. You actively listen to their concerns, showing this by nodding and making acknowledging sounds. You calmly explain the returns policy while remaining assertive and offering a resolution for the customer.

You might not consider this an interpersonal skill, but the very fact that you have listened, been patient and helped to resolve the situation is a demonstration of your interpersonal skills. Even if you haven't had any work experience, you will still be able to provide evidence of this skill; think about your studies.

Example: As part of your course at school, college or university, you are required to give a group presentation.

Four of you are in the group; one member refuses to undertake a certain aspect of the work, and others complain that they are not pulling their weight. You decide to try and resolve the situation. You spend time listening carefully to the other members of the group, and you avoid getting drawn into negative conversations with your peers. You help resolve the situation by offering a few solutions, such as changing duties or negotiating deadlines, and as a result your group successfully finishes the tasks and presents their presentation to your class.

This type of situation is renowned for causing conflict. In this situation, you may have tried to help and listen to other members of the group, empathise with the different participants and help resolve the conflict. You will have used your interpersonal, negotiation and teamwork skills in both situations.

Customer orientation: You can meet the customer's needs in a flexible and friendly manner. The words you can use to describe yourself in this situation are welcoming, approachable, listener, tactful, diplomatic and anticipator.

Example: If you work in or have worked in retail, hospitality or a customer service environment, while you may not have heard of this term, you will certainly have this skill set.

You have worked in a retail setting, selling arts and crafts products, for example, books, cards, pictures and ornaments. Your manager encourages all new members of the team to spend time getting to know about all the goods that are on sale, for example, who the maker is and what the story behind the item is. Each week, you review any new items in stock and extend your knowledge of the shop's range. You even create a brief reference guide you can access. The time and knowledge of the goods become invaluable; you can speak to new customers and find out their requirements, are interested in a specific theme, such as sustainable goods and their values, and then use your knowledge to anticipate their needs and provide a better customer experience and service.

Verbal (spoken)/written communication: You can communicate both formally and informally, whether that be verbally face to face, online or via telephone or in writing, such as email, letter, produced online content, for example, website or social media. This could be within employment or within a small or large employer, both internally and externally. Outside employment, you could correspond with campaigns for change and write to politicians, organisations and so on. The words you can use to describe yourself in this situation are communicator, content writer, influencer, orator or skilled communicator, narrator, speaker and presenter.

Example: You will have examples of your verbal communication skills from many aspects of your life, both working, studies and/or social. If we refer to the examples above, both the teamworking and interpersonal skills examples will include verbal communication skills. In a work or study situation:

You will have concisely explained your thoughts and ideas when you worked with your team members to create the Christmas promotion in the store and/or when working with your peers on a group project. In both these situations, one of your team members or peers may have to ask probing or open-ended questions and spend time listening, repeating or paraphrasing aspects of what you heard to clarify your understanding of what was said. These are all forms of verbal communication.

Example: We probably don't realise that you use your written communication skills daily. If you are working, then you should have lots of examples to draw from.

You have been working in an administrative role and created a new process for dealing with email correspondence. Your office keeps an operational manual where all new processes are stored as a reference point from which new members of staff can learn. You create a new document for the process, laying out the rationale for the process and procedure and outlining the steps in a clear format for others to follow.

Example: You work as a volunteer for a local charity and have been asked if you can help with their social media presence or create content for their website to increase volunteer applications.

You volunteer at a local charity and have experience with social media, for example, Facebook and Instagram, and creating content for websites. You spend time reviewing the current social media presence and website, understanding the tone and type of messaging used. In addition, you review what other charities are using in the social media campaigns. You write some text, initially getting your ideas down and spending time editing the message and ensuring it is concise, on point, and has the right tone. You seek feedback from others in the organisation before designing and creating a social media campaign and adding additional content to the website.

Example: If you have no paid or voluntary experience to draw from, you will still be able to evidence. If you have been studying – school, college or university – then you will have examples to draw from here.

You have been working on your assignment; this could be an essay or dissertation. You have spent time researching your essay using accessible web search engines such as Google Scholar. You create a plan for your essay before you even set pen to paper; you may have used a mind-mapping tool that helped you capture and organise your ideas and information. Once you have written your first draft of your essay, spend time rereading it, ensuring the essay is concise and that you have used the appropriate tone and language, as well as checking your spelling and grammar. You finish your essay and/or dissertation and gain excellent marks and feedback on your style, tone and content from your teacher or lecturer.

Cultural awareness: You can understand the differences between yourself and people from different countries and backgrounds, including the differences in attitudes and values.

Example: If you are in paid or voluntary work, you should be able to produce evidence of cultural awareness.

You work part-time in a local farm shop outlet, and the owners are of a different religion from yours. During your time working there, you come to understand and appreciate their religious beliefs. They do not open the business on Sundays, as this is part of their beliefs. This example shows how you do not have to travel to another country to gain cultural experience. There are many examples you can consider evidence of this skill whether you are in the UK or further afield.

As a student at school, college or university, you will be studying with other students from many different backgrounds and cultures. You can use your day-to-day experiences as evidence of this skill, or if you have or are preparing for a placement, then you may have an example like this:

Example: As a university student, you may have a placement abroad:

You are a university student and hoping to study abroad as part of your course. As part of your preparation, you spend time improving your language skills and learning some common phrases to help you during your time in Germany. As part of your preparation, you attend a session at your university on working in Germany. This session covers cultural norms for the country, ethics towards work, and workplace etiquette. Your placement in Germany and preparation for your trip have improved your cultural awareness, and working in Germany has also given you global acumen skills.

Global acumen: the ability to work with different people, consider situations from various perspectives, and have cross-border collaboration skills and intercultural awareness.

Example: Above we covered an example of cultural awareness from a placement in a different country, this example could also evidence your global acumen skills.

On your placement in Germany or even a graduate on an internship, you are going to work for a local company; in your role, you are working alongside team members who are German and French. Before you go to Germany, the company arranges online Teams meetings to get to know the team before you arrive. You are teamed up with another colleague from Germany and set some initial tasks before you arrive. You work on a project to promote the service in Germany, and you come together and discuss your colleagues' cultural differences. You take time to understand the various perspectives of your colleagues, as well as the different cultural norms, such as work etiquette and working hours. Working remotely before you arrive improves your cross-border collaboration skills, and you gain awareness of time scales, for example, an hour. You finish the project and receive feedback on this and our placement, which acknowledges your global acumen and skills.

Example: However, you don't have to travel or work in a different country to demonstrate this skill set. You may be a member of a club, church or community group.

In your spare time, you are a member of a local community group. The charity aims to support new people coming to live in the area, ensuring people know about service and other charities that can support them. In your role, you help with the food bank and work alongside other volunteers who have different cultural backgrounds, for example, other volunteers who have settled in the UK. In your roles, you work together to get food donations from local people and businesses and meet and greet people when they arrive at the food bank. Through your role, you meet many people who were both born in the UK and have backgrounds different from yours or those outside the UK. Weekly, you all meet as a team and discuss issues and cultural barriers to accessing the service and listen to other perspectives on how to break down barriers to accessing the service. This type of example also is a demonstration of cultural acumen, cultural awareness and so on.

It is important to have a better understanding of the meaning of skills and transferrable skills, and hopefully, the section above will help you with that. I recommend that you audit your skills using the 'Employability skills audit tool' (shown below), try doing so initially without the skills dictionary. In this way, you will get a sense of those skills you are unsure of, then go back to the ones you have struggled with, for example, interpersonal skills read the definition and the examples, then return to the audit tool and I am sure you will realise you have this skill and will be in a better place to provide evidence for your covering letter, CV, application form and interview.

Employability skills audit tool

People skills	Study	Work (paid or unpaid)	Your examples and evidence
Teamworking			
Leadership			
Interpersonal			
Customer orientation			
Oral/written communication			
Cultural awareness			
Global acumen			

Remember you can download the audit tool by following the QR code or using the URL at the start of this book; on viewing it you will see several key transferable skills on the left, and you can decide where you have gained that skill, such as study or work, and then provide an example.

IN A NUTSHELL

This chapter aims to help you consider what to include when you're a first-time, part-time or graduate applicant. When writing these types of letters, it is essential to remember:

- Use the basic ingredients and create three to five paragraphs.

- Spend time considering your unique selling points, as well as understanding and auditing your transferable skills.

- Tailor your letter with the relevant audience in mind, for example graduate employer.

You can access the activities via the QR code and URL at the front of this book and download the 'Employability skills audit tool' and 'Skills dictionary'. This can help you further understand your transferable skills and USP. If you would like to do some further reading on how to tailor your covering letter not only to the role you are applying for but also to different career trajectories, turn to the back of the book for further reading suggestions and resources.

7 DISCLOSING AND SHARING SENSITIVE INFORMATION

So far, this book has shown you how to write and structure your letter to promote yourself and your skills, qualifications and experiences. But there may be other information you wish to share with the employer that you believe is pertinent to your application and therefore should be discussed earlier rather than later. Some of this information could be deemed sensitive or personal but important for the employer to know.

This chapter will cover a wide range of topics, but not all will be relevant to everyone. They have been written to enable you to dip in and out, reading only the topics that are appropriate to you. Within each topic, additional websites and support resources have been listed to enable you to find out more if desired.

The topics covered within this chapter are:

1. age;
2. caring responsibilities;
3. criminal convictions;

4. disability, including long-term illness, mental health and special needs;
5. neurodivergence;
6. gaps in work experience;
7. gender reassignment;
8. sexual orientation;
9. religious beliefs;
10. right to work in the UK.

Age

How old you are is not something that is commonly mentioned in either your CV or covering letter. This is because age discrimination laws make it unlawful for any employer to treat an applicant differently due to their age. If they want to, an employer will be able to get a rough idea of your age based on details in your CV, such as what year you left school or graduated, and the number of years of work experience you have.

There are, of course, exceptions to most rules, and age is no different. There are some roles which do carry restrictions regarding the age someone needs to be to carry them out, within the law, this is called an 'occupational requirement'. For example, anyone under the age of 18 is not legally allowed to serve alcohol, and employees are required to be between the ages of 18 and 60 to be a police officer or firefighter due to the physical demands of the job. Employers cannot just decide this for themselves, though; for it to be a genuine occupational requirement, it must be all of the following:

- crucial to the post, and not just one of several important factors;

- relate to the nature of the job **and**

- be 'a proportionate means of achieving a legitimate aim'. If there is any reasonable and less discriminatory way of achieving the same aim, it is unlikely the employer could claim an occupational requirement.

Even though it's not necessary to include your age in your CV, it's entirely up to you if you choose to mention it in your covering letter. The main reason to mention it is if you think it will add to the reasons why an employer might want to interview you. Remember, your covering letter is a tool to help convince an employer to invite you for an interview. There is no need to include anything that won't help you to do this.

Some people think that if they are 'too old' or 'too young' that this could count against them in the recruitment process. But your age could be the exact thing that counts in your favour.

Older candidates

If you are an older candidate, reasons that may put you off disclosing your age could include:

- You think it may put you at a disadvantage against younger candidates.

- You believe you only have a few good working years left before retiring, and the employer is probably looking for someone who will stay with them for a long time.

- You're embarrassed to be job searching at your age.

- Others may perceive you as being out of touch with current trends and technology.

69

According to an employment survey by the legal recruiters Douglas Scott, the average length of time people stayed with one employer was four years and five months. Interestingly, 'the length of time a person spends in a role increases significantly the older they get, with people 25 and under only spending, on average, three years in a position. By contrast, people aged 58 and over, spent just under seven years in a role.' These survey results debunk the first two points on the list above.

Your age should be seen as something to shout about because:

- it demonstrates depth of knowledge and skill;

- your problem-solving skills have been tried and tested and refined to a fine art;

- you are less likely to need time off due to childcare or parental responsibilities;

- you'll have a larger network of potential customers, contacts or collaborators;

- continuously seeking to climb the career ladder may be less important to you than loyalty to the employer;

- skills, including adaptability, flexibility, resilience and being able to cope with change, are things that you will have many years' experience of.

Do not belittle all those years of studying, working, networking and learning. Instead, be proud of it and use it to your advantage.

An example sentence could look like this:

Throughout my working life I have had the opportunity to continuously update my IT skills and have on occasion mentored newer members of staff on the companies' CRM system.

This demonstrates that instead of being old and out of touch, you have kept up to date with technology and supported the learning of others, demonstrating coaching, mentoring and teamwork skills too.

Younger candidates

As a younger candidate, you might feel this will put you at a disadvantage because:

- you lack the years of practical experience others may have;

- you will lack credibility, and older workers may not listen to you or take you seriously;

- you're suffering from 'imposter syndrome' and therefore believe that everyone else is far better qualified than you are and you don't deserve to be offered the job;

- you think you'll be viewed as someone who is just there for the money and isn't planning to stay long.

In fact, according to a study by PivitolHRCanada, younger people are loyal to their employers, but what is driving them to move jobs is the financial hardship they are facing. If there were better benefits packages and transparent routes for training and progression, it's likely that younger workers wouldn't move on so quickly.

So, what do you have as a younger person that you can highlight in your covering letter?

- Younger people tend to bring fresh ideas and perspectives that may not have been previously considered.

- As a generation that has grown up with technology at their fingertips and is familiar with the fast pace of technological development, younger people are often more confident and excited to try new things.

- You are ready to get started on your career journey and are eager to learn.

- There's a higher chance that you don't yet have multiple responsibilities, such as a mortgage or children, therefore enabling you to be more flexible in your working hours. You may also be more willing to relocate for a job, thus eliminating a long commute.

All these things are attractive to an employer, so don't be ashamed of your lack of experience; instead, be proud of what you do have.

An example sentence could be:

> I am excited to get started on my career journey and combine my graphic design skills with my extensive imagination to produce high-quality product designs for ABC Creatives.

This shows a keenness to get started, fresh creative ideas and technical skills.

Caring responsibilities

It is a common misconception that you can only include skills gained through paid or voluntary employment in your CV and covering letter. But the fact is, an employer is seeking someone with the required skills and doesn't mind how they gained them. If you have had caring responsibilities, you will no doubt have accumulated a multitude of skills including time management, resilience, patience, communication, organisation, problem-solving, empathy, multi-tasking and decision-making. All these are highly sought after by employers, so should be mentioned either within your CV or covering letter.

Remember that the covering letter needs to be tailored to the role you're applying for, so think about all your experiences and match these to the skills, experiences and abilities the employer requires.

It is easy to undersell yourself and what you have achieved. Just stating that you've had caring responsibilities for X number of years, while being true, isn't giving the whole and accurate picture. Instead, you might say:

> While caring for an elderly relative, I took financial responsibility by ensuring all their bills were paid on time and in full. I effectively liaised with professionals, including social workers, medical staff and pension providers, to deliver accurate and prompt provision of services to my relative. I did this while working and studying part-time, thus demonstrating my excellent time management and organisational skills.

Criminal convictions

If you have any criminal convictions, it can be a cause of anxiety when applying for a job. Hopefully, this section and the accompanying resources will help to put your mind at rest about how to disclose should you decide to, or because your conviction is unspent, you need to.

The main point to make is you do not need to disclose a criminal conviction until you are asked. Employers sometimes put this as a question on application forms, or they may ask during the interview process. You can choose to wait until this time before disclosing, or you could pre-empt this question by disclosing it in your covering letter. Remember, your covering letter is a means of convincing an employer to invite you to an interview, so anything you write here should be with this aim in mind. You should be prepared to discuss at the interview anything you disclose in your covering letter.

Whatever the reason for the criminal record, you must be honest about it because, if you are dishonest, it will be this dishonesty that may result in your not getting or losing the job rather than the criminal conviction itself.

A covering letter should always be tailored to the job you're applying for, so this will impact whether you need to mention a conviction. For example, if you're applying for an office-based job and have driving convictions, they are unlikely to negatively impact your application and probably aren't worth mentioning at this time.

If, though, your conviction is unspent, this will need to be disclosed. Remember, though, the employer is still mainly looking at whether you can do the job and will fit in with the team. So, rather than focusing on any negative aspects related to the conviction, focus on the positives, which could include:

- achieving useful qualifications while in prison;

- having a job in prison has provided you with skills the employer needs;

- providing you with time to reflect upon your career journey and being more focused now;

- having improved your skills in teamwork, problem-solving, resilience and punctuality.

If you are concerned about how and when you need to disclose a conviction or need support to help you find employment, there are a few organisations available to support you. The main two in the UK are Unlock and Nacro. Look at their websites to learn more.

Disability, including long-term illness, mental health and special needs

According to the law, you are considered to have a disability if you have a 'physical or mental impairment which has a substantial and long-term adverse effect on their ability to carry out normal day-to-day activities (i.e. not just their job activities). For instance, some individuals with depression or anxiety find rush hour travel on public transport unbearable' ('Disclosing a Mental Illness in the Legal Workplace' | LawCare).

Disclosing a disability is very personal, and it is not a legal requirement. It is important to note that you can choose to disclose your disability at any point in the recruitment process, so spend time thinking about when you feel most comfortable. If you have disclosed your disability on your CV, you can use the fourth paragraph of the covering letter to provide additional information about yourself and your disability. You could add the additional skills you have gained through your experience of disability, such as perseverance, problem-solving, resilience and patience, highlighting your lived experience and how you have overcome barriers. You could outline potential reasonable adjustments. For example, if you are deaf, you may want to consider requesting that the employer contact you via email or text rather than phoning you.

Whilst disclosure of a disability is a complex and personal decision to make, if you are a BSL user, it is useful to disclose this on your cover letter – as an interpreter will need to be booked. The employers may wish to discuss the logistics of undertaking an interview with an interpreter – especially if they have not worked with an interpreter before. You should always request a fully qualified interpreter in order to feel confident about the process. (Lynne Barnes, Academic Lead, BSL & Deaf Studies)

See the quote above for an example of what adjustments you may request if you are a BSL user. Remember, you can disclose your disability at any point during the recruitment process, and the quote below reminds you of how and when you might disclose.

> *Disclosure is a very personal thing, and no matter when and where you choose to disclose it must feel right for you. Sometimes you may choose to disclose at the onset of you application i.e. to gain a guaranteed interview via the Disability Confident Scheme, and other times choose to disclose when offered an interview to ensure any reasonable adjustments i.e. extra time in online tests i.e. psychometric tests. There are no hard and fast rules, but this is an area you could talk through with a careers adviser. (Elizabeth Dinse, Freelance Career Coach, Disability and Higher Education)*

Neurodivergence

If you are one of millions of people who is neurodivergent, you have numerous skills, strengths and qualities that many employers will appreciate.

Sadly, according to the Institute of Occupational Safety and Health, despite almost one in seven people being neurodiverse, in a 2023 survey, '72 per cent said they would either not declare it on a job application or were unsure if they would do so'.

It is not a legal requirement for you to disclose your neurodiversity within your covering letter, but if the employer is made aware of it, they can put things in place to support you, not only during the application and interview process but also once you are working for them. Without the knowledge of your neurodiversity, the employer will be unable to support you, and you may not, therefore, be able to show off your full potential.

The Association of Graduate Careers Advisers (AGCAS) has produced a leaflet which provides some useful phrases you can use when writing your covering letter. This covers neurodivergences including ADHD, autism, dyspraxia, dyscalculia, dyslexia and Tourette's Syndrome.

Here is an edited version of one of the examples from the AGCAS leaflet:

> I have a neurological disorder that sometimes causes difficulties with concentration, sitting still and impulsiveness. This means I have strengths in certain areas, including having quick reactions and being a creative thinker, and I can improvise in a difficult situation.

This example is one that could be used by someone with ADHD. In the leaflet, further strengths are listed. I would advise choosing two or three to use in your sentence and tailoring these to the job description.

Gaps in work experience

If you are worried that an unexplained gap in your work experience may put an employer off inviting you to an interview, you could add an explanatory sentence in your covering letter. You do not need to go into a lot of detail at this point.

What is the definition of a gap? For some employers, if the gap is less than three to four months, it's not worth worrying about or mentioning. If the gap is over four months, then you should be prepared to explain it. This does not necessarily need to be on your CV or in your covering letter; it could instead be during an interview if you are asked. If the gap wasn't recent, it's also not usually worth mentioning. Employers are more interested in what you have been doing recently and the skills, qualities and qualifications these activities have resulted in which will make you an asset to their workplace.

There are many reasons why you may have gaps in your employment, such as, being made redundant, seeking work, caring responsibilities, having children, returning to study, travelling, illness or a prison sentence.

It is illegal for an employer to discriminate against anyone due to their health status, and this includes discriminating due to a health-related gap in their employment history.

Regardless of the reason, every instance will have provided you with the opportunity to gain or improve upon certain skills, and it is these you need to focus on when writing an explanation in your covering letter. For example, if you were unable to continue working due to an illness, while receiving treatment and recovering you may have been keeping up to date with industry news, using the time to reflect upon your career journey or completing online study courses.

A gap in employment does not have to be a negative thing to be ashamed of. It may be that you chose to prioritise yourself and your health and well-being, which is why you chose to take a break from working. You may have decided to go travelling, do an extended period of volunteering, or simply take a break to prevent burnout. All are valid reasons, and all should be celebrated rather than hidden.

Whatever the reason for the gap in employment, you must be honest about it because, if you are dishonest, it will be this dishonesty that may result in your not getting or losing the job rather than the gap in employment. Remember, your covering letter is a positive record of your achievements and is used as a tool to convince an employer to invite you to an interview.

Mentioning a gap in employment in your covering letter could look like this:

> Before starting at university I took a year out to work and travel. I was pleased to be able to use (and improve) my language skills — French in the Far East and Spanish in South America. I spent some of the time travelling alone which exposed me to local culture and developed my self-reliance and resilience. I also did some casual work, in a bar and a hostel, while in Australia. (Prospects.ac.uk)

If the role you're applying for is the first one after having a career break, you might say:

> I'm returning to work after taking a career break to raise my children. During this time, I was spending valuable time with my children before they started school. I developed numerous skills, including resilience, patience and how to juggle multiple tasks simultaneously. I also became very adept at problem-solving, thinking on my feet and remaining calm under pressure. These are all qualities I believe would enable me to carry out this role to a high standard.

This situation puts you at an advantage as it is likely that you'll be available to start work immediately, while those in employment will need to work their notice period first.

If your employment gap was due to a mental or physical illness, you do not need to disclose the precise details of the illness itself. You could simply say:

> Because of a long-term/recurring health condition, I was unable to continue in my previous employment. After a period of recovery, I am ready to take the next steps in my career.

Gender reassignment

Gender reassignment is a protected characteristic under the Equalities Act 2010, and therefore it is illegal for any employer to treat you differently because of gender reassignment. This relates to any person who is planning to undergo, is currently undergoing or has undergone gender reassignment.

You may feel that it's necessary to refer to your gender reassignment in your covering letter because you have legally changed your name or are known by a different name than that which appears on your qualification certificates, for example. However, disclosing in your covering letter is purely optional and depends on how comfortable you feel doing it at this stage. Your covering letter is a place to promote your skills, qualifications and achievements that you believe make you an excellent candidate for the job. You do not need to mention anything that doesn't fulfil these criteria. Your gender identity, gender reassignment and possible change of name only need to be known by the HR manager within the company, as it has no bearing on your ability to do the job.

If you chose to undergo surgery related to gender reassignment, you may have needed time off work. You may therefore decide to explain the gap in employment alongside the reason for this, but only if you are comfortable doing so. Remember to always focus on the positive attributes that you have demonstrated, such as resilience, positive mental attitude and determination to succeed.

Do not feel pressured into disclosing anything that you are not comfortable doing.

Sexual orientation

According to the Equalities Act 2010, 'It is against the law to discriminate against anyone because of their sexual orientation.' As with many other things in this section, disclosing your sexual orientation to a potential employer is entirely optional. What you need to consider is why you feel that it would be important or necessary to disclose and how you would do it.

Some people view their sexual orientation as something that needs to be kept hidden or something to be ashamed of. The reasons why they feel it necessary to hide it include:

● fear of discrimination;

● fear of bullying and harassment;

● fear of not being employed or being dismissed from a job.

You'll see the word 'fear' mentioned numerous times here. Sadly, according to a CIPD report, '40% of LGB+ workers and 55% of trans workers in the UK have experienced such conflict, compared with 29% of heterosexual, cisgender employees. A higher proportion of LGB+ workers (16%) feel psychologically unsafe in the workplace compared with heterosexual workers (10%), while for trans workers, this figure is even higher at 18%.'

With these figures in mind, why would anyone want to disclose their sexuality in a covering letter? Here are a few reasons:

- Many employers recognise that if an employee is having to hide who they are in the workplace, they are not being as productive as they could be. So, by coming out to them early on, you are showing your dedication to being a fully productive member of the team.

- Employers are trying to improve their workplaces for LGBTQ+ employees. By applying to them, you're indicating that they are moving in the right direction and prompting them to keep going.

- The job you are applying for may benefit from your unique lived experience, and by disclosing you are improving your chances of being employed.

- By the employer's response to your application, you'll learn quite quickly whether they are an inclusive employer, and this will help you decide if you want to work for them.

Whatever your reasons for sharing your sexual orientation, it's important to do so professionally and appropriately. Here are a few examples:

In my last role, I was chair of the LGBTQ staff network, thus enabling me to improve my communication, organisation and networking skills. I also developed great event planning skills when I planned a World AIDS Day awareness fundraiser, which raised over £1,000.

As a member of the LGBTQ+ community and Stonewall role model, I feel perfectly placed to support the young people your organisation works with, especially those who may be questioning their gender identity or sexuality.

Volunteering for the LGBTQ+ support line has opened my eyes to the struggles faced by LGBTQ people every day. It has greatly improved my communication and listening skills and empowered me to work harder to strive for equality for all. I believe this job at your company will give me a great opportunity to do that.

Religious beliefs

The UK is a culturally diverse country, and this is certainly true when it comes to the religious affiliations held. A report from the UK Deed Poll Service cited at least 26 different religions mentioned by its applicants. These include the more common ones such as Christianity, Catholicism, Hinduism, Judaism, Buddhism and Sikh as well as lesser-known ones such as Zoroastrianism, Wicca and Shamanism. Mentioning your faith or religion within your covering letter is an entirely personal choice. What you need to consider is why and how you would share it.

The main reasons why you may decide to share your religious beliefs within a covering letter could be because, once employed, you may require time off for religious observations and events, or you may need certain accommodations to enable you to practise your faith.

How you mention it could be combined with other things such as voluntary work with or for your local place of worship, having been involved with a religious society while with a previous employer, or a proud achievement such as being chosen to do a reading in front of a congregation. What this will demonstrate to the employer is your community spirit, interpersonal skills, leadership and public speaking, among other things.

Example sentences include:

> While volunteering as a leader at my church youth group, I was responsible for the planning and implementation of a range of fun activities for the young people to participate in. This pushed me out of my comfort zone a little but enabled me to grow in confidence and self-belief whilst developing my leadership and organisational skills.

> I was honoured to be chosen to deliver a reading from the Torah on Shabbat. As the first female in my family to be chosen to do this, I felt the weight of expectation upon me. I was proud of how I calmly and clearly delivered the reading, demonstrating dignity, humility and the ability to remain calm under pressure.

Right to work in the UK

When applying for a job, it's important to the employer that you are legally allowed to work in the UK. It could be that you currently live in another country and are applying to work in the UK, or it could be that you already live here but all your previous experience has been in other countries. It's best, at an early stage, to set the employer's mind at ease, that you have the appropriate visa allowing you to work and that you don't require sponsorship.

You don't need to go into a lot of detail within your covering letter, and if you're able to combine it with something else, even better. For example:

> As a US citizen, I am very much looking forward to experiencing UK culture. Having obtained the correct working visa, I do not require sponsorship and am excited to start work as soon as I can.

This lets the employer know you have the right paperwork and that you are available to start work soon without needing to serve a notice period.

Remember to include within your covering letter any strengths you bring as an applicant who has worked, lived or studied outside of the UK, which could include:

● language skills;

● experience of other cultures;

● independence;

● ability to cope with change.

In Chapter 6, 'One Size Doesn't Always Fit All', you'll find more information about applying as a European or international applicant.

IN A NUTSHELL

This chapter has covered a range of topics, but a few things have cropped up several times, including:

● For many things, mentioning it in your covering letter is a personal choice rather than a legal requirement.

● Remember to always tailor your letter to the job. When mentioning any of the topics from this chapter, do so only if relevant and within a sentence highlighting what you can bring to the role.

● Most of the topics in this chapter are protected characteristics, so you are protected from discrimination through the Equalities Act 2010.

● Be honest about anything you choose to share in your covering letter.

● If you need more support, there are a range of specialist organisations willing to help.

8 OTHER WAYS OF USING A COVERING LETTER

SPECULATIVE APPLICATION, NEGOTIATING OFFER, RESIGNATION AND PROMOTION

Throughout this book, the message is not to use the same covering letter for every application. Tailoring your letter to make the most impact and stand out from the crowd is essential. It is important, therefore, to remember that 'One size doesn't always fit all' (see Chapter 6). Once you have created your covering letter, it is not written in stone, and just like your CV, it is a living document that should be tailored, changed and updated for each application. However, once you are more confident with your covering letter, you can use the formula to write further letters for other reasons.

This chapter will discuss in more detail the different types of covering letters, such as speculative, negotiation, resignation letters and promotion.

This chapter will help you:

- understand what a speculative letter is, when and how to use and create one;

- when to use a negotiation letter and what to consider before you put pen to paper;

- what to write in your resignation letter to end your employment on a positive note;

- understand what to include in a promotion letter or expression of interest.

Speculative letters

As a career adviser in HE, I often spoke to students and graduates about creating a speculative letter. Many had yet to hear the term and were unaware of what it was or how to use this type of approach.

Before exploring what a speculative letter is, it is essential to realise that not all jobs are externally advertised; they may not appear on job search sites or job pages.

Have you heard of the term 'the hidden job market'? Some employers have vacant posts and recruit candidates by word of mouth and/or reputation. The reality is that not all jobs are advertised externally. In fact, according to the University of Surrey (2023), 'up to 80% of job opportunities may not be advertised'. This might shock those new to the job market and job searching, but the term describes this aspect and helps you realise that thousands of jobs go unadvertised. In the quote below, read about the benefits of a speculative approach and get some first-hand tips.

A speculative cover letter is an excellent opportunity to showcase your experience and skills to an employer for a 'hidden job' and one that is not necessarily advertised. A well-written letter can tell employers a lot about an applicant, including your qualities, values and, hence, your fit with their business. In addition, it can also demonstrate your interest in their company and your writing skills, in terms of your ability to accurately articulate what you have to offer, such as your professional skills, knowledge and experience.

A few important tips, I often suggest to students and graduates include using a good structure, consider the format e.g., a formal letter, or informal message, tailor it to the employer, and include skills and information relevant to the role(s) you can do. When choosing skills, it's useful to research these using job profiles on careers website such as Prospects, or National Careers, and use a STAR method example to evidence these. Use AI to help research the company only and always check the letter for spelling and grammar. (Andrea J Atherton, Careers and Graduate Employability Adviser, UCLan)

Top tips on accessing the hidden job market

If you are unsure where to start, here are a few tips on accessing the hidden job market.

Current employer: As an employee, you already have access to internal vacancies. These will usually appear on your company vacancies pages; however, if there is a specific department you are interested in, you could try to network with colleagues in this area. Some employers offer opportunities to shadow colleagues in another department. This allows you to network, build relationships with other colleagues and team leaders, demonstrate your skills and abilities, and hear firsthand if an opportunity is about to arise.

Expand your network: Expanding your network is important, and by doing so, you can hear firsthand about opportunities and market your USP to a wider audience. If you do not have a LinkedIn account and profile, this would be a good time to create one. Now, if you need help figuring out where to start, there are many great resources in the public domain. LinkedIn has its how-to guides, that is, creating a LinkedIn profile that opens doors; alternatively, if you are attending high school, college or a university, they might have their resources to help you get started. If you need help figuring out where to start, look 'Further Reading and Resources' chapter. Once you have your profile, you can follow and connect with others in your career areas, join groups and so on. If you identify someone doing the job role you aspire to or someone who is a recruitment manager, sending them a connection request and a message is also good practice. Here, you could use a short version of your speculative letter, explain your interest in the company or role if you seek advic and so on. Suppose you are interested in a specific company. In that case, you can also use your LinkedIn or other forms of social media, such as Instagram, X (formerly Twitter), and Facebook, to research the company and who works there. This information then can be used to know whom to address your speculative letter to gain insight into the company and help with the content of your letter.

I know graduates who have used Instagram to follow casting companies and hear firsthand about internships, placements and jobs being highlighted. Using your social media is another way to get noticed by companies. Just a word to the wise: if you are going to use your Facebook and other social media platforms, consider what you post, types of pictures and images, as companies will be able to see more of your personal information, so it is worth checking your privacy settings and being mindful of what you post. Consider setting up a separate social media account as part of your job-searching strategy.

Professional bodies and organisations: Your chosen profession may also have a professional body. Many years ago, when I started my PhD, I became a member of several career professional bodies. This enabled me to hear about events and conferences relevant to my sector. I made several connections through presenting at conferences. This expanded my network massively and resulted in numerous opportunities over the years that followed, such as publishing. Word of mouth is a powerful tool; it is often underestimated and undervalued. Many professional bodies have student memberships, so do not be discouraged if you have not completed your studies.

Now you realise there are thousands of jobs and opportunities unadvertised. It's time to make the most of a speculative approach.

This is where the speculative letter approach comes into its own. However, here is a warning: do not think you can write one generic letter and expect results. In my experience, those students who do best with this approach:

● create a job search strategy;

● research the companies they wish to contact;

● create a tailored individual speculative letter and CV for each application.

I've seen many students adopt this approach. They researched the companies that appeal to them, either because of their specialism or other criteria outlined in their strategy, for example, location. They then tailored their CV and speculative letters, and those who took a very measure approach were successfully invited to interviews. The basic ingredients of your covering letter will remain similar; see Chapter 2, 'Understanding What Should Be in Each Section'. However, the main change will be in paragraphs one and two.

Introduction to you and why you are writing

This time, you will not have seen a formal advertisement; you are speculating and making a speculative approach. You still need to start by introducing yourself, for example, 'I am a third-year computer design student at the University of XXX'. Then you need to explain the purpose of your letter, and why you are sending it, for example, I am looking for an internship or placement with ComputerX.

Why are you the best potential applicant?

Like writing a covering letter, your second paragraph is where you highlight why you are a potential applicant. You must highlight your skills and experiences and link these statements to your tailored CV. You will not have a job specification to help you identify what to include in your letter, so do some research and look at 'job profiles' on either Prospects or the National Careers Service, both will outline the qualifications and skills needed for specific roles.

Why are you applying to them?

You must also include a paragraph highlighting why you chose them, outlining your career aspirations and interests and mentioning why you contacted them and their recognition in the sector. This is where your research is important, and it is equally important to make it relevant to you as an applicant. You can include a range of topics:

- business values, mission statements;

- their work with local communities, charities and so on;

- awards, such as Investors in People;

- part of the Stonewall Diversity Champions Programme, or Disability Confident Scheme.

If you don't know anything about the employer, research them; often, their website and LinkedIn can help you in your research.

When writing your covering letter, supporting your claims with evidence is important. You can use a few methods to support this, namely STAR.

What does STAR stand for?

S = **Situation** – Identify the SITUATION or problem you solved or encountered.

T = **Task** – What was the TASK you accomplished (who, what, when, where and so on).

A = **Action** – Detail your ACTIONS (what did you do, how did you do it).

R = **Result** – Explain the RESULTS (include numbers, quality and costs and savings).

You can use this approach in several ways, such as covering letter, CV, application form and interview. Why use this method? When you are providing evidence of your skills and or experiences, just stating 'I have excellent communication skills' is vague, it has no depth and doesn't provide insight for the reader into how you have or delivered this skill. This is where the STAR method comes into its own and helps you formalise your evidence and statements. For further examples of STAR and telling the STAR story, look at Chapter 10. If you are struggling to recall evidence of your skills, see Chapter 6. You can use the skills audit and collate where your examples come from, for example study or work (part-time, paid or volunteering).

The first three paragraphs are key; this is where your research will pay off. The remainder of the speculative letter follows the same format as the covering letter. Provide additional information, make your closing statements and sign off on your letter. See examples in Chapter 2.

Below is an example of how to set out your speculative letter:

Template for a speculative letter

Your address
Phone number
Email address

Name of person, for example, Mr Taylor
Job title
Address

Date

Dear Mr Taylor

First paragraph: Introduce yourself and explain your background, for example, 'I am a third-year computer design student.' State why you are writing, for example, 'I am looking for an internship with ComputerX and wondered if you had any placement or internship opportunities.'

Second paragraph: Link the letter and highlight your experience on your CV, for example, 'In my attached CV, you can see I have experience in JavaScript and have recently completed the shortlist for Young Web Developer of the Year.' Further, highlight **why you are the best potential applicant** and showcase the other aspects of your skills, including transferable skills and experiences that would appeal to the employer you are writing to.

Third paragraph: Highlight your knowledge of the company you are applying to and give examples of its reputation, area of expertise and so on, for example, 'From my research, I know ComputerX is recognised for its innovations in the computer sector.'

Fourth paragraph: This paragraph is optional; it is for **additional information**. You could note additional skills and experiences from a gap year and so on, and share and disclose information such as a disability, for example, request a reasonable adjustment or alternative form of communication.

Fifth paragraph: This is your **closing statement;** here, you are rounding up your letter, telling the employer you look forward to being called for an interview, noting your availability or holidays and so on.

Yours sincerely/faithfully

NB: Type your name if you are sending the letter electronically.

The section above provides a template to help you write your covering letter. While the example above focuses on the sender using a speculative approach to explore opportunities, that is, an internship, this type of letter could also be used if you want to contact an organisation for example, a charity to explore voluntary opportunities. You may wonder why you would consider voluntary work and to be honest, I have heard many students say similar as this type of work is unpaid. However, as a volunteer, you will be paid in so many other ways not to mention gaining skills, work experience, adding to your CV and gaining a reference. Volunteering also provides you with the opportunity to test out your career aspirations and, guess what, employers look very favourably on those who volunteer. The speculative letter, like the covering letter, is yours; therefore, you need to make it personal. Think about your USP (unique selling points).

Negotiating offer letter

You may have already been through the process of applying for a job, and you get that call or letter saying the employer wants to offer you the post! This is brilliant news; however, maybe the salary offered is on a scale that is less than your current salary. Or the terms and conditions are different from what you were hoping for. What do you do? Some job seekers will accept the new salary or terms and conditions, but it is OK to negotiate with the new employer. You can do this over the phone, by email or by letter. If you intend to write an email or a letter, this section will help you think about what you need to consider and include. This type of letter is known as a 'negotiating offer letter'.

Once you have confirmation that you have been offered the post, contact the employer, express your interest and ask for some time to consider their offer. It is perfectly acceptable to do this.

How to write a negotiating offer letter

By now you should understand the importance of preparing yourself and spending time researching the employer when writing your covering letter. Equally, here, you need to take some time to consider the offer that has been made and how the role will aid you in achieving any career plans you have.

Take some time and consider the following points:

- What is your career plan? Where do you see yourself in the next five years?

- Does the role you have been offered fit into that plan?

- Is it a promotion or a sidestep?

- What will be the impact of the salary and terms and conditions?

- Does the salary reflect what is being offered across the sector?

- How qualified are you?

Once you have done this, you will have a clearer understanding of whether you can accept the job offer as it stands or not. In a time of a cost-of-living crisis, every penny is important. It might be hard to believe employers expect you to negotiate your salary after the initial job offer. It is estimated that 70% of employers expect this, but still, less than half of us do this when offered a job (Science of

People, 2024), and Milkround (2024) states many employers expect you will negotiate your salary.

Who is paying what

Do some research and see what other companies are offering for the same role:

- Review job search sites, such as Indeed, Prospects, Milkround and Jobs.ac.uk.

- Access salary guides, for example, Reed and Hayes produce a downloadable salary guide, which includes data on salary bands and the average salaries for specific sectors, such as accountancy and finance.

- Review your current salary and be aware of your salary banding.

Most organisations have what is known as salary bands. These are set out by a company based on their education, job specification, duties, experience and so on. Indeed (2024) explains an employee in an administrative role:

> May have differing levels of experience and authority, so they would each be part of salary bands corresponding to the work that their role entails.

Below is an example of salary bands for local authority jobs (2023):

Grade	SCP	Scale point	Salary	Salary
G001	SCP0001	5	£23,500	£27,582
	SCP0002	6	£23,893	£27,975
	SCP0003	7	£24,294	£28,376
	SCP0004	8	£24,702	£28,784
	SCP0005	9	£25,119	£29,201
G002	SCP0006	11	£25,979	£30,061

NB: The table above is an extract from the Local Government Association pay and grading structure.

So, if you are already employed, you could also review your current pay, see where your pay is on the salary band and scales, and ascertain if you will be due for a pay rise or what is often referred to as a pay increment. This could also give you a benchmark against which to review the new job offer pay and give you further evidence for your negotiation offer letter.

What might you be worth

It's also important to consider your selling points and worth. If this is your first job, it can be harder for you to ascertain. However, if you already have a job, you have a benchmark salary and more skills and experiences to draw on.

Below are some points to consider:

- Have you been studying recently? Do you hold a good range of GCSEs, a diploma or BTEC, an undergraduate degree in a specific subject or a master's and a PhD?

- Think about your skills and experiences. These do not just have to come from paid employment. If you volunteer for a charity or are involved in sports or clubs, these can all be sources to draw from.

- Do you belong to a professional body, hold professional qualifications, for example, an undergraduate degree in counselling and a member of the BACP, or have a qualification that is part of the allied health professionals, such as podiatrist and occupational therapist, and registered to the Health and Care Professions Council (HCPC).

The basic ingredients of your covering letter will remain similar, see Chapter 10. However, the main change will be in paragraphs one and two.

Introduction

This time, you have the job offer in hand, so you need to start your letter by acknowledging this, expressing your interest in the post and thanking the employer for the offer.

Outline your new proposal

If you have followed the steps above, you will now have the information you need to draft your new proposal. Start by reminding the employer what qualifications and experience you hold, outline your current or average salary from your research, and then state your new salary proposal. Follow a similar format if you ask for changes to your working conditions, such as a day to work from home or a varied week. You may be asking for these changes due to caring commitments or to balance your health or a disability. You could also review the company's policies in these areas to support your request or ask for these changes as part of a reasonable adjustment.

Considering the terms and conditions

Many people might write a negotiation letter because the salary does not meet their expectations. As said earlier, in a cost-of-living crisis, every penny counts, and you need the best salary you can get. It might be the case that you are content with the salary. However, the terms and conditions are not what you wanted, for example, you may have benefited from hybrid working, working remotely from home, a day a week or you worked a condensed week, that is, longer hours four days a week and off one day a week. You may have a disability that you have or haven't yet disclosed and wish to negotiate and request a reasonable adjustment with the employer's flexible start and finish to help work around your condition.

The remainder of the letter follows a format similar to the cover and speculative letter. You could include an additional paragraph for additional information. Remember, it is important to close your letter and thank the employer for their time and offer.

Below is an example of how to set out your negotiation offer letter:

Template for a negotiation offer letter

Your address
Phone number
Email address

Name of person, for example, Mr xxxx
Job title
Address

Date

Dear Mr Taylor

First paragraph: Start your letter by thanking the employer for the job offer, such as 'thank you for offering the position of Computer Designer at ComputerX', and acknowledge your appreciation for their time and for being shortlisted.

Second paragraph: Outline your proposal for a new salary or conditions. Reiterate your qualifications and experiences and a willingness to negotiate the salary offer further, for example, 'In my current role, my salary is at £xx,xxx, and this year, I would be due my next increment taking my salary to £xx,xxx. I have x years' experience, and already hold qualifications in JavaScript, therefore would you consider the revised salary of £xx,xxx?'

Third paragraph: This paragraph is optional; it is for **additional information**.

Fourth paragraph: This is your **closing statement**. Here, you round up your letter, remind them of your interest and thank them for their time.

Yours sincerely,

NB: Type your name if you are sending the letter electronically.

> *Negotiating a salary can be a tricky area, and the main piece of advice links to one of the most critical skills that employers are looking for — commercial awareness. Before negotiating any salary, you need to do your research into the general salary expectations for the role, the employer and wider market — there are lots of ways you can do this, for example online research, but also speaking to professionals in the industry. Being prepared will put you in a better position to address any specific questions from employers. Salary, however, is only one part of the picture, and any discussions need to be balanced with your motivation for the actual role. If you're not able to negotiate the salary you want or expect, will this role still help you with your career goals? Will it offer you growth and development opportunities? Again, preparation will help you make a more informed decision. (Monira Ahmed, Careers Consultant (arts and law))*

The section above outlines what you should consider if you are thinking about writing a negotiation letter. The quote reiterates that it is not always easy to write this type of letter and what you need to consider.

Resignation letter

You may already be employed in your first job, a part-time or full-time role, or a more substantial role. Either way, you still need to write a resignation letter to your current employer when you plan to resign. When writing your letter and leaving an employer, it is always best to write it on a positive note.

Even though you are resigning, you still need to take some time, consider the contents and do some research.

Check your contract
When writing your resignation letter, it is important to check your contract. You might wonder why! You will have signed some specific terms and conditions in your employment contract, such as notice period. Before you put pen to paper, check what you agreed to. It could be a week or months. Giving up to three months' notice in some sectors is not unheard of.

Holiday entitlement

Most people's annual leave runs over 12 months, but each employer is different. For example, in the education sector, holidays run from September to September, while other employers may go from April to April. So, find out if you have any holidays left. Also, decide if you want to take them before you leave or use them as part of your notice period. Alternatively, you could request the employer pay you for any leave you are owed in your final salary.

The basic ingredients of your resignation letter will remain similar. However, the main changes will be in paragraphs one and two, possibly three, if you want to provide additional information.

Introduction and resignation

In this paragraph, start by stating that you wish to give notice of your resignation. Remember to state your job title and reiterate the name of the employer.

Outline your notice period

You have done your research and know what is expected concerning your notice period. Here, outline it and state your last working day. You can also request that your human resources department confirm this is correct.

Holiday entitlement

You should also now know if you have any holidays owed. As stated above, you could add to the paragraph above and state that you wish to use the holidays owed as part of your notice. Alternatively, you could write an additional paragraph asking the employer to pay you for any holidays you are due.

The remainder of the letter follows a similar format to the other letters in this chapter. You could include an additional paragraph for additional information, and you still need to close your letter.

Below is an example of how to set out your resignation letter:

Template for a resignation letter

Your address
Phone number
Email address

Name of person, for example, Mr xxxx
Job title
Address

Date

Dear Mr Taylor

First paragraph: Start by stating to your employer you wish to resign, for example, 'Please accept this letter as notice of my resignation from my position of Computer Designer at ComputerX'.

Second paragraph: Repeat to the employer what your **notice period** is, for example, 'As my notice is four weeks, my last working day will be 20 May 2024.'

Third paragraph (optional): If you have accrued leave and will not be taking it as part of your notice, ask the employer to pay you your **holiday entitlement** in your final salary, for example, 'I believe I am accrued 5 days leave and request this is paid as part of my final salary.'

Fourth paragraph (optional): You may want to add some **additional comments or information**, such as thanking them for their time and support during your employment.

Fourth paragraph: This is your **closing statement**. Here, you round up your letter, remind them of your interest and thank them for their time.

Yours sincerely/faithfully

NB: Type your name if you are sending the letter electronically.

Promotion/expression of interest letter

You may be in a position where you are aware there is a promotion opportunity, or you should be considered for promotion. In this situation, you may consider writing a promotion letter, otherwise known as an 'expression of interest'. This type of letter has similarities to the other covering letters outlined in this chapter. However, this time, you are highlighting why you should be considered for promotion or an upcoming opportunity.

Timing is everything

It might also be worth checking out the overall status of the business you're working for before you start, that is, if there are restructures or redundancies expected, as this may mean you consider waiting until another time. Consider having a conversation with your manager before you send the letter; then, if you have verbally expressed your thoughts and/or interest, it won't be like your 'cold calling' and a total surprise.

Outline your request

As with all the other letters outlined in the chapter and book, it's important to be professional in your tone and consider the language used. Look at Chapter 4 if you need a reminder. The first paragraph of your letter should start by thanking them for taking the time to consider your request, for example, the promotion, state your current role, and then the desired role. Remind the reader of how you have been working towards this opportunity; an example could be that you have been undertaking extra duties, for example, supervising others. Present the facts and note your interest in the promotion opportunity.

Remind the employer of your USP

In the second paragraph, it is important to remind the employer of your knowledge of the skills and experiences required for the role. Then, you should present an example that demonstrates the skills required. Additionally, if you have undertaken any training or qualifications or had positive feedback over this period, consider how you can add this evidence. Start by drafting out your thoughts, making some notes and then using STAR as a format to write the sentences and paragraphs. If you need a reminder of what STAR is or some examples of how to write a sentence in this format, look at Chapters 8 and 9. Here, you can also add how you are aware that if you gain the promotion, this may leave a gap in the team. Present your thoughts and ideas on how you could support this transition or help train other team members.

Additional information and closing statements

If you have anything further to ask or state, you could include a third paragraph, for example, if you were due to take leave, you could offer to delay it into the next holiday entitlement year. However, this paragraph is optional, and you can use it as and when you need to. In the final paragraph, take the opportunity to thank the reader for their time and for considering your request for promotion, you could add if they have any further questions that you are open to chat these through with them in a meeting.

Template for a promotion letter

Your address
Phone number
Email address

Name of person, for example, Mr xxxx
Job title
Address

Date

Dear Mr Taylor

First paragraph: Start by stating that you would like to thank the employer for considering your letter, for example, 'Thank you for taking this time to consider my request' and set out your reason for writing, such as, 'I am writing to formally request a promotion from computer designer to the role of senior computer designer'.

Second paragraph: Acknowledge your awareness of the skills and experiences needed for the new role, for example, 'I know the role of senior computer designer requires a specific skill set, including supervising the team'. Then, give an example of this, for example, how you supervised the team while covering the role, or note any extra training you have undertaken.

Third paragraph: This paragraph is optional. However, if you leave to take, you should also acknowledge that you are aware of the impact of taking leave and note you would be happy to carry any leave over into the next holiday period.

Fourth paragraph: This is your **closing statement**. Here, you are rounding up your letter, thanking the employer for their time and considering your request. State that you are open to arranging a meeting to discuss your request could be implemented.

Yours sincerely/faithfully

NB: Type your name if you are sending the letter electronically.

IN A NUTSHELL

This chapter has focused on different types of covering letters, such as speculative, negotiation, resignation and promotion letters. When writing these types of letters, it is important to remember to:

- create a researched and tailored speculative letter;
- research the job market and know your worth when writing a negotiation letter;
- check your notice and holiday and resign on a positive note;
- outline your knowledge of the promotion role and highlight how you have what's needed.

If you want to do some further reading on how to use the covering letter as a speculative, negotiation, resignation and/or promotion letter, turn to 'Further Reading and Resources'.

9 DIGITAL VERSUS PAPER LETTERS

We live in a digital age where almost anything and everything can be sent electronically, but sometimes it might be worth considering what some may call the old school approach. When was the last time you printed or even handwrote a letter and posted it to someone? For many, I suspect this is a rare occurrence.

If you are applying for an advertised role, the employer may have stated the way they'd prefer to receive your application, in which case you need to follow these instructions. But, if you are applying speculatively, you often have the freedom to decide for yourself. View every step of the application process as an opportunity to showcase your personality as well as your strengths and abilities. If you think that submitting a neatly handwritten letter will impress the employer, then do it. If, though, you think they'd be impressed by your digital submission, then do that. Finding these things out is all part of the process and, if you get it right, you will get the employer's attention in a positive way.

Unfortunately, you might find yourself in a position where you are finding it hard to apply digitally due to what is termed as 'digital exclusion' and this could be, according to a report by the Centre for Economic and Business Research, for one of a few reasons, including:

Access – not everyone can connect to the internet and go online.

Skills – not everyone can use the internet and online services.

Confidence – some people fear online crime, lack trust, or don't know where to start online.

If this is the case, a handwritten letter could be your only option. But it may be worth speaking to the staff at your local library, as they usually have computers that are free for the public to use and often run basic computing courses. For example, on the Southampton City Council website it says: 'Our libraries have computers free to use for library members, free Wi-Fi at most sites and printing, photocopying and scanning facilities', and, the City of Edinburgh Council says: 'Library members can use the internet and Wi-Fi, scan documents and use Microsoft Office software in all libraries.'

Submission instructions

Examples of instructions informing you how to apply include:

- To apply for the position, please select the **'Apply for this job'** button at the bottom of the page.

- Applications must be submitted in a single PDF file that includes three parts in the order of:

  - a covering letter;

  - a current CV, including date of birth, country of citizenship and highest degree level;

  - contact details for three references.

- For our roles, apply using a C.V. and covering letter or complete the online application form.

If you are looking at vacancies on a site, such as LinkedIn or Indeed, clicking the 'apply for this job' button may take you to an online submission area where it may ask you to complete a form or upload your CV and covering letter, or it may take you to the employer's own website where they will provide instructions on how to apply.

These instructions are very specific, so you need to ensure you follow them precisely.

These instructions give you the option of a form or a CV and covering letter, so you can choose your preferred option.

But what if you're sending a speculative application and therefore there are no instructions? What options do you have? This chapter will cover these options, the pros and cons of each as well as providing hints and tips on email etiquette and letter writing protocol.

Letters

Not many people write formal letters anymore, but during the job application process, it is one occasion where you might be expected to. Once you've written the letter, you have the choice of whether to print it and either hand-deliver or post it or add it as an attachment with your CV to an email.

Regardless of which delivery method you choose, you still need to consider how your letter is laid out on the page. In Chapter 8, you'll find several letter templates that show you how to lay one out. But let's run through it in detail.

Layout

At the top of the page, ideally on the right-hand side, you should put your name and contact details along with the date. You do not necessarily need to include your address, but you should include at least two different forms of contact details, such as email and phone or email and address. It's important to remember to include the date after your contact details so that the employer knows exactly when you sent the letter. These should be properly aligned with the edge of the page.

Aligned to the right ————————→

Mrs Jane Smithers
1 Crown Crescent
Stationville
ST01 V23
Jsmithers1@ggmail.com
07123 987654
18th January 2025

Under your address, aligned to the left-hand side of the page you should have the address details of the person you are sending the letter to. These should be 1 line below the date. The addressee is always on the left as this is where the window is located in windowed envelopes, which some organisations use.

←———————— Aligned to the left

Mrs Linda Jones
Personnel Manager
Jones Marketing Ltd
24 Great Street
London
W14 9LK

Name of addressee(s)

Whenever possible, in both the address and when starting the letter, you should try to find the name of the person you are sending the letter to rather than just using their position or job title, for example, the Personnel Manager or Chief Pharmacist. This helps ensure that the letter gets straight to the correct recipient rather than doing the rounds of in-trays until it eventually, hopefully, gets to the right person.

To start the letter, you need to use the person's name again rather than saying 'Dear Sir/Madam' or 'To whom it may concern'. For example,

Dear Mrs L Jones or Dear James Robinson

There are several ways of finding the correct person to address your letter to, including:

- Look at the job advert to see if it mentions someone specifically to address your letter to.

- Look at the company profile on LinkedIn to see if you can find the appropriate person.

- Phone the company and state that you are planning to send in your CV and letter and ask who should you address it to.

Pronouns

Never be tempted to guess someone's pronouns. There will always be some names which you come across on a regular basis and others which are less familiar to you. This can leave you with the temptation to assume or guess at someone's pronouns. Do not do this, as it may cause unnecessary offence or discomfort to the other person. It is better to leave off the pronoun entirely than to make an incorrect assumption.

If the person has sent you an email, they may have included their pronouns within their email signature or, if they have a LinkedIn profile or similar, they may have added their pronouns there. If you're not sure, take a minute or two to check, as this can alleviate any future embarrassment if you get it wrong.

Stating the purpose

Below the addressee, you'll need to state the purpose of your letter; this is much like the subject line of an email.

Re: Administrative officer vacancy

If in the advert they have provided a vacancy code or number, always mention this within the subject line, for example,

Re: Administrative officer vacancy (AO123)

The body of your letter should be laid out in paragraphs as shown in Chapter 8. You will then sign off using either 'Yours sincerely' or 'Yours faithfully'. This is called the salutation. Your signature follows this, with your name written underneath it.

Yours sincerely

J Hanley

Mrs J Hanley

Yours sincerely or Yours faithfully?

This is the bit that confuses some people: which sign off is appropriate to use at the end of your letter. The general rule is 'Yours sincerely' is used when addressing someone by name, while 'Yours faithfully' is used when starting with 'Dear Sir/Madam' or similar.

Dear Mrs Smithers
Yours sincerely

Dear Sir/Madam
Yours faithfully

If you forget which is which, you will always be safe using 'Yours sincerely' at the end of a letter, as this is the preferred sign-off in business or formal letters generally.

Pros and cons of a printed letter

If you plan to post your letter with your CV to the employer, there are some obvious cons to this, namely:

- The cost of postage, paper and an envelope.

- The time that it will take to be delivered, especially if it's going abroad. Be aware of application deadlines and be sure to post your application so that it arrives on time.

- The uncertainty of when and if it's been received – you may want to consider sending it by registered mail so you can track its progress, but this will cost more.

- Upon receipt, it may sit in someone's pigeonhole or in-tray for a few days before being opened. If the intended recipient is on leave, it may not be opened for a few weeks.

- If handwritten, the employer may struggle to read your handwriting.

What are the pros of a posted letter?

- It looks professional and, if laid out properly, it should impress any employer.

- You can design and format it to match your CV.

- If handwritten, you may impress the employer with your neat and professional handwriting.

- It's a more personal approach, which some employers appreciate.

- As few people do it, it'll help you stand out from the crowd.

Rather than posting your letter, if the company is local, you may choose to hand-deliver it. The cons of this method would include:

- The time and effort it would take to do this.
- Possible transportation costs to get to the company premises.

The pros of this method are all those listed above under the pros of a posted letter, as well as:

- You know it has arrived at its intended location safely.
- It's quicker than posting, and you won't need to pay for postage.
- The employer should be impressed by the effort you have taken to apply to work for them.
- If they're available, you may be able to hand it directly to the intended recipient. (If this is a possibility, remember to dress to impress, as first impressions count.)

Emails

Sending an email is fast, free and convenient, making it the preferred option for many people. In the submission instructions, the employer may request that this is how you submit your application.

It can be a dilemma whether you write your email in the style of a letter and attach your CV to it, or whether you write a very short email and attach both your covering letter and CV to it. Some employers may state their preference in the submission instructions, whereas others will leave this up to you. Ultimately, it doesn't make a huge amount of difference. As long as there is a covering letter and a CV, whether it is in the body of the email or attached is not usually a deal breaker.

Covering letter as an email

If you decide to write your covering letter within the body of the email, you will set it out exactly as you would a letter, but without the addresses as these aren't necessary. Even though this is an email and not a letter, you need to keep the same level of formality as a letter. Do not fall into the trap of being too informal, as this may not go down well with the employer.

Starting your email with 'Hi', 'Hello' or any other informal greeting is unacceptable, as is 'Cheers' or 'Thanks' at the end.

Covering letter attached to an email

If you decide, or are asked by the employer, to attach your covering letter and CV as separate documents to an email, you need to remember to add a line stating what you have attached and what role they relate to.

Your email may read a little like this:

Dear Martin Smith

Re: Admin Officer vacancy A123

Please find attached my CV and covering letter for the administrative officer role as advertised in the Daily Echo on 23 May.

Yours sincerely,

Sarah Green

File name

Remember that first impressions count, and this even comes down to what you have named the file containing your CV and covering letter. It needs to be short, simple and professional. You may have named it 'my super awesome covering letter for my dream job updated version 5' when you were writing it; this now needs to be changed to something more suitable. The file name should tell the recipient:

- what it contains;
- who it is from;
- the date it was updated or written (whichever is the most recent).

Avoid including any blank spaces. You may have seen when something you have written as S Green covering letter is translated into S%20Green%20cover%20letter. This is because some applications don't recognise blank spaces, so they fill them with %20. To avoid this, use underscores (_) or hyphens (-) instead. So now we have 'S_Green_cover_letter_May_24'.

The best length of a file name is between 25 and 35 characters, which includes the underscores or hyphens. The example above contains 27 characters, so it is within the optimal range.

You should also avoid using punctuation, symbols or special characters such as &~,$.*¥Ω|\. This is because special characters in file names can cause compatibility issues with different operating systems and applications. Some characters might have specific meanings or functions within certain operating systems or programmes, which could cause errors when used in file names. Helpfully, if you attempt to use certain characters when saving a

DIGITAL VERSUS PAPER LETTERS

document, your computer will often let you know if you have used something that isn't allowed and will prompt you to change it.

File type

You can create your document in Word, but when attaching it, it's best to save it as a PDF first. You can do this by going to 'File' clicking on 'Save As' and selecting 'PDF' from the 'Format' drop-down menu. The advantages of sending your covering letter and CV as PDFs include:

● They are less likely to attract viruses.

● They are more secure than Word documents.

● The formatting remains the same regardless of what device or programme is being used to access them.

But some employers still prefer you to submit these documents as Word documents because:

● They take up less storage space due to usually being smaller than PDFs when compressed.

● Word documents can always be read by ATS, whereas as older ATS may not be able to read some PDF files, especially if they have been saved as an image file. (See Chapter 10 to learn more about ATS.)

● If you're applying through a recruitment agency, they may want to edit your covering letter and CV before sending them on to an employer, they can only do this if you've sent it in Word.

Pros and cons of emailing your covering letter

Emails are the quickest way to get your covering letter to the intended audience, but there are some downsides to this method too.

Cons of emailing:

- An email is very impersonal.

- Your email may get placed in a spam folder and, unless they look, could be missed by the recipient.

- The formatting and layout of an email may change or become distorted on different devices.

- An email is easy to write, and there's the danger that you click submit before you have checked it properly.

- Your CV and covering letter may contain personal information about you, which you might not want to send in an email due to privacy concerns.

- Employers receive many emails daily, and yours may get missed.

- Consider timing as well as time zones. You don't want your email to land in the middle of the night or on the weekend so that by the time Monday rolls around, your email has been buried under a pile of newer ones.

Pros of emailing

- It's fast and free.

- It's good for the environment as it reduces paper waste.

- You can attach multiple documents in addition to your CV and covering letter, such as a portfolio or a personal statement.

- It's convenient.

IN A NUTSHELL

- Always follow the instructions given by the employer on how to submit your CV and covering letter.

- If you have a choice, use the method that will help you stand out from the crowd in a positive way.

- Always tailor the letter to the job and the role, and how you choose to submit the letter is no exception.

- Regardless of the submission method used, keep it polite and professional.

10 STYLE AND SUBSTANCE

Hopefully, by reading this book, you'll have realised that the most important part of any covering letter is the words you put in it. But once you've got this sorted, you might want to look at adding a bit of creativity to your letter.

You will already have seen in Chapters 2 and 9 how to lay out a professional-looking letter on the page, but you might decide to spice this up a bit by demonstrating your creativity.

If you decide to be creative in your letter, always keep at the forefront of your mind that because the words in the letter are the most important part, it is imperative that the recipient can read them. You can have the most beautiful-looking letter, but if the words can't be read, it's pointless.

You also need to bear in mind that not every employer will appreciate a creative letter, so carefully research the employer before deciding what your letter will look like. More traditional employers will probably prefer a standard professional letter without any additional design elements, whereas a small start-up company or creative employer may well appreciate the effort of making your letter look more appealing.

What is the purpose of adding design elements?

There are several reasons why you might want to add imagery or design features to your covering letter, including:

- to illustrate parts of your personality;
- to show off your design skills;
- to help your covering letter stand out from the crowd.

But if you don't get it right, you could stand out for all the wrong reasons.

Here are a few top tips to help you.

1. Keep it simple and be selective in choosing imagery and design elements. You don't want your letter to look so busy and full that it distracts from the letter itself. This is not your portfolio, so you don't need to show off everything you can do at this point.

2. Use the imagery to demonstrate relevant skills. If you are adding things you have designed, drawn or photographed yourself, choose items that will demonstrate skills required for the job you're applying for. There's no point in showing off your fine art skills if you won't be asked to use them in the job.

3. Consider using colours, shapes and fonts that reflect those used by the company you're applying to. Doing this will show the employer that this covering letter has been designed specifically with them in mind. They should appreciate the time and effort you have put into it, and hopefully this will translate into you being offered an interview.

4. Keep it clean. Regardless of whom you are sending it to, you need to ensure you have not included any artwork or imagery which could be offensive, embarrassing or crude. Most employers will not appreciate receiving this from a candidate.

5. If appropriate, think about designing your own logo and including it on the letter.

6. Keep it to one side of A4. Regardless of what you're adding, you should still keep your covering letter to one side of A4.

Personal branding

What is personal branding and how does it apply to your covering letter?

No, a personal brand is not a new form of tattoo! Your personal brand is everything that makes you, you.

If you think of any well-known brand, be it a company or a person, there isn't just one thing that defines it; there are many things tied together to make that brand. Take IKEA for example, according to their website, they are:

> a global home furnishing brand that brings affordability, design and comfort to people all over the world. We may have come a long way since our humble beginnings, but our vision remains the same: to create a better everyday life for the many people.

Some people, when they picture IKEA, will think of the striking blue and yellow IKEA sign; others will picture furniture; whereas some will picture the flat-pack instruction booklets. It isn't any one of these things on their own that make IKEA's brand; it's all of them combined.

Can a person have a brand though? The simple answer to this is yes, of course they can. A perfect example is Sir Richard Branson, the founder of the Virgin Group, who has created a brand that blends entrepreneurship with adventure. His personal brand conveys that risks can lead to innovation and that business should be fun and adventurous. Branson's brand is also entwined with his beliefs in social responsibility and making a positive impact in the world.

What, though, does any of this have to do with a covering letter for a job? Your letter, as well as providing factual information about you, also needs to communicate to an employer what your personal brand is all about. To be able to do this, you need to have a clear idea yourself of what your brand says about you.

Take a few minutes to answer these 10 questions.

1. What are your career goals?
2. What makes you unique?
3. What are your core values?
4. What are your top strengths and weaknesses?
5. How do you want other people to see you?
6. What do you care deeply or are passionate about?
7. What motivates you?
8. What's your favourite thing to do in your spare time?
9. If you were to receive an award, what would it be for?
10. What's the weirdest or quirkiest thing about you?

Perhaps team up with someone and ask them to read the questions to you out loud so that you can answer them as if you're in a job interview. This way you are forced to think about them on a deeper level. Ask the other person to answer the questions about you and see if your answers match, especially question 5 which asks about other people's perception of you. It can be quite revealing, and sometimes humbling, to learn how others see you. The answers to all these questions are what makes up your brand. Now all you need to do is package it all up and think of a way to write and present your letter so that your brand is accurately portrayed! Easy right? No, not really, so here are some top tips to help you.

1. **Use colours** – not just because you like them but because of what they mean. Traffic lights have taught us that red means stop or danger. But what else does red stand for? According to Adobe, 'Red is a very strong colour with associations both positive and negative. On the positive side, red symbolises strength, passion and confidence. But it can also be aggressive, symbolising anger, alerts or danger.' Every colour has meanings tied to them, and you need to consider these when adding colour to your personal brand. If you are an active, upbeat person who is full of energy, you might want to add splashes of yellow and orange to your brand, whereas calm, loyal people might go for shades of blue and purple.

2. **Carefully choose your font** – according to Canva, there is something called font psychology which is 'the study of how different fonts impact thoughts, feelings, and behaviours'. Most fonts fall into different categories, including Serif, Sans Serif and Script. Serif fonts include Times New Roman, Garamond, Baskerville, Georgia and Courier New. These fonts communicate trust, respect, authority and formality so they would be a great choice if this fits with your brand and you are applying to a more traditional job role or company. Sans Serif fonts include Arial, Helvetica, Proxima Nova, Futura and Calibri and are often associated with something or someone that is straightforward, modern, sophisticated or cutting-edge. Finally, Script font examples such as Monotype Corsiva, Lucida Calligraphy, French Script, Coronet and Brush Script

are altogether fancier and portray emotions including creativity, happiness, whimsy and sophistication. Which font you use will be instrumental in helping you communicate your personal brand, so choose carefully.

3. **Be authentic** — by creating a brand for yourself that doesn't truly reflect who you are and what you are all about will not help you in the long term. Don't pretend to be something you're not just to get a job. Employers will value authenticity over fabrication every time. Plus, you may be able to keep up the act during an interview or even after starting a job, but in the long term, this will be much harder and end up negatively affecting your productivity rather than supporting it.

4. **Tell a STAR story** — wording your letter in such a way as to make it read like a story will help to make you and your letter more memorable for the employer. If you think about how a story is structured, it will have the scene setting, the challenge or main thing that occurred, how the challenge was overcome and the resolution. If you've learnt about answering interview questions, you may have heard of the STAR approach. Storytelling is a little like the STAR approach but with a few added bits. STAR stands for situation, task, action and result. Your story will build around these basics, but you can also include challenges that occurred, how you emotionally felt before, during or after and what the relevance to the employer would be.

    For example: 'Whilst working at the supermarket I had to stack shelves' could be 'Whilst stacking shelves at the supermarket I was challenged with making the displays look tidy, well organised and stacked correctly according to expiry dates. My introductory training had covered all of this and although I initially made a few mistakes, I felt proud when my manager said I'd done a really good job. I feel that I can use this experience to good effect within the role of store assistant at . . .'

This mini story expresses the following things:

- Determination to succeed.

- Attention to detail.

- Pride in doing a job well.

- Organisational skills.

- Ability to learn from mistakes and not give up.

- Ability to apply what has been taught.

- Relevance to the job being applied for.

- And the fact that this person had worked at a supermarket stacking shelves!

This is far more interesting to read than someone just listing these qualities. Another quote you'll often hear in relation to storytelling is 'show don't tell'. So don't just list what you can do; surround it with narrative and make it into a mini story instead. Read more about the star approach in Chapter 8

5. **Keep it simple** – however you choose to make your letter stand out while promoting your personal brand, keep it simple. If you decide to add images, icons, designs or colour, don't go over the top with these as this can make your letter appear cluttered, disorganised and overwhelming. Hopefully, this is not what your personal brand is all about!

6. **Be consistent** – for a personal brand to be effective, it needs to be consistent everywhere it is seen or heard. Your CV, which will be accompanying your covering letter, should be laid out in the same style and using the same fonts. Your professional social media pages should use the same or a similar style of content throughout, which complements that used in your CV and covering letter. If an employer sees bright, brash colours and

lots of capitalised or underlined words in your LinkedIn profile, yet your Instagram is all pastels and script fonts, and the letter they are reading is in Sans Serif and laid out in a very formal manner, they are going to be quite confused as to what you are like and what you can bring to their company and the job. Put yourself in the employer's shoes and then Google yourself. What message would the employer be getting about you and your personal brand? If you were to answer the 10 questions from earlier in this chapter based on the results of the Google search, would they match up with your earlier answers or contradict them? Now add your CV and covering letter into the mix. How do they compare with your Google search results?

When you are at the start of your career journey, it's relatively easy to set everything up to look authentic and consistent. However, if you are further into your career journey, you may already have a personal brand that you are known by. Or, you may have inadvertently put out mixed messages by not being consistent on all your social media pages. This is harder to change but not impossible. The sooner you are aware of what your personal brand is, the sooner you can start working on ensuring all your forms of communication are consistently promoting it, which includes your covering letter.

Creative covering letter examples

If you are not a designer or artist but still want to portray your creative, playful or quirky side in your covering letter, there are a few simple ways to do this. If you create your letter using a Word doc, when you click on Word, don't click on the 'Blank document'; instead, choose from 'search templates'. Type in covering letter or creative covering letter, and it will provide you with a range of options and designs to choose from. These can all be edited to suit you and your brand. Here are a few examples:

ABOUT ME

I am an aspiring graphic designer with an eye for the unusual and unique. With exellent knowledge of Adobe Creative tools I am keen to start my career journey.

CONTACT

@ someone@example.com

📱 07700 987654

🌐 www.example.com

Manchester

📍

[Recipient name]
[Title]
[Company]
[Recipient Street Address]
[Recipient Town/City,
County, Postcode]

JUDE HANLEY
TRAINEE GRAPHIC DESIGNER

Dear Mx Slater,

I am excited to apply for the Trainee Graphic Designer position at Great Designs R Us that I saw advertised on Indeed. I recently completed my Graphic Design degree at University of Anytown and gained practical experience during a summer placement at Anytown City Art Gallery, where I designed promotional materials and social media graphics.

My skills in Adobe Creative Suite, combined with my passion for creative design, make me eager to contribute to your team. I admire Great Design R Us for its innovative work and would love the opportunity to learn and grow as part of your team.

I would appreciate the chance to discuss my application and talk through my portfolio with you.

Thank you for your consideration.

Yours Sincerely,

J Hanley

Mrs J Hanley

[3a Gordon Place]

[telephone]
[tel]
[email@address.com]

[24th June 20XX]

[Arthur King]
[Store Manager]
[Great Foods Supermarket]
[123 High Avenue]
[anytown]
[GK12 4XX]

Dear Mr King

I am writing to express my interest in the Sales Assistant position at Great Foods Supermarket, as advertised in the local newspaper. With a strong background in customer service, cash handling, and stock rotation, I am excited about the opportunity to contribute to your team and ensure an excellent shopping experience for your customers.

In my previous role as a Sales Clerk at Minimart, I gained hands-on experience in assisting customers with their inquiries, processing transactions quickly and accurately, and maintaining well-organized and stocked shelves. I have developed a keen eye for detail, which helps me ensure that products are correctly labelled and displayed in a way that maximizes sales. My ability to engage with customers in a friendly and professional manner has consistently contributed to positive feedback and repeat business.

Key skills that I bring to the Sales Assistant position include:

Customer Service: Providing personalized assistance to customers, resolving issues, and ensuring they leave the store satisfied.

Cash Handling: Accurately managing cash transactions, balancing tills, and ensuring the security of all financial operations.

Stock Rotation: Implementing effective stock rotation practices to minimize waste, keep shelves full, and ensure products are fresh and readily available.

I am a dedicated and reliable team player, always willing to go the extra mile to support my colleagues and contribute to a positive work environment. I am confident that my experience and passion for providing excellent service align with the goals of [Supermarket Name].

Thank you for considering my application. I am eager to discuss how my skills and experiences can benefit your team. I am available for an interview at your earliest convenience and can be reached at [Your Phone Number] or [Your Email Address].

Yours Sincerely,

Liz Dinse

Jane Browne

Ms Sharon Michaels
Sharon's Flower Basket
Green Lane
Berkshire
BE1 7F3

18/07/2024

Dear Ms Michaels

I am excited to apply for the Experienced Florist position at Sharon's Flower Basket. With 8 years of hands-on experience in floral design, customer service, and retail management, I am confident in my ability to contribute to your team and create beautiful, bespoke arrangements that delight your customers.

In my previous role at Flower Power, I was responsible for designing and arranging floral displays for various occasions, including weddings, corporate events, and everyday orders. My expertise in working with a wide range of flowers and materials, coupled with a keen eye for colour and design, allows me to craft arrangements that are both visually stunning and aligned with customer preferences.

I am particularly drawn to Sharon's Flower Basket because of your reputation for unique and artistic floral designs. I am eager to bring my passion for floristry and dedication to customer satisfaction to your team.

Thank you for considering my application. I look forward to the opportunity to discuss how my experience and skills can benefit you.

Your Sincerely,

J.Brown

Mrs Jane Browne

16 Border Creek
Portsmouth
Hampshire
UK
PO94 8TP

023 30777999

jb@ggmail.com

JaneBrowneFlowers.co.uk

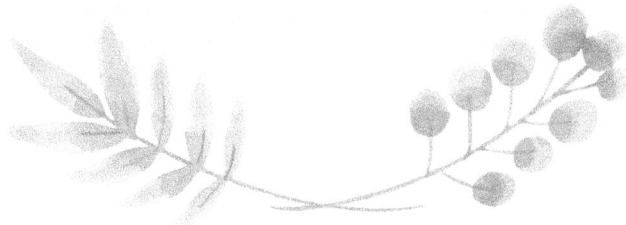

Additionally, sites such as Canva or Google Docs provide excellent alternatives to Word.

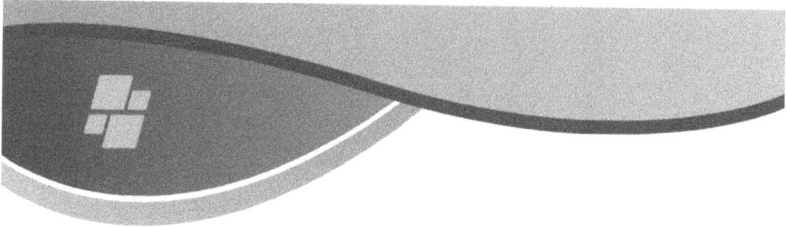

20 July 2024

Dear Matt Zhang

I am writing to express my interest in the entry-level Estate Agent position at Zhang & Co. With a background in office administration and customer service, I am eager to begin my career in estate agency and contribute to your team's success.

In my previous role as an Office Administrator at Grant, James & John, I developed strong organisational and multitasking skills, managing daily office operations and ensuring a smooth workflow. My experience in customer service has equipped me with the ability to communicate effectively, understand client needs, and provide exceptional service skills that I believe are essential for a successful career in estate agency.

I am particularly drawn to Zhang & Co because of your reputation for excellence and your commitment to providing comprehensive training for new agents. I am enthusiastic about the opportunity to contribute to your team and grow my skills in the property market.

Thank you for considering my application. I would welcome the opportunity to discuss how my background and skills can benefit you.

Sincerely,

Jamie Chastain

+123-456-7890
+123-456-7890

www.reallygreatsite.com
hello@reallygreatsite.com

123 Anywhere St.,
Any City, SO12 345

BRIGITTE SCHWARTZ
MARKETING ASSISTANT

123 Smith Street
Cardiff
UK
CF1 234

12 June 2025

Miss Selina Markus
BBS
Main Street
Cardiff
UK

Dear Selina Markus,

I am writing to apply for the Marketing Assistant position at BBS. With two years of experience in marketing, I have developed a strong foundation in campaign management, content creation, and data analysis. I am particularly excited about the opportunity to contribute to your online marketing efforts.

In my previous role at Samco, I played a key role in executing successful online marketing campaigns, including social media management, email marketing, and SEO optimization. My hands-on experience has honed my ability to engage target audiences and drive measurable results.

I am drawn to BBS because of your innovative approach to digital marketing and am eager to contribute my skills to help achieve your goals. I would welcome the opportunity to discuss how my background aligns with your needs.

Thank you for considering my application. I look forward to the possibility of contributing to your team.

Your Sincerely,

Brigitte Schwartz
Applicant

☎ 123-456-7890   ✉ brigette@example.com

Alex Jamieson
123 Your Street
Your City
Gr18 678

4th August 2026

Ronny Reader
CEO, Jamleys
24 Address Street
Your City
GR18 6AB

Dear Ms Reader

I am writing to apply for the part-time Stockroom Assistant position at Jamleys. As a recent school leaver, I am eager to begin my career and believe that this role would be an excellent opportunity to develop my practical skills whilst contributing to your team.

While I may not have formal work experience, I have developed strong organisational and time-management skills through my studies. I am hardworking, quick to learn, and highly motivated to take on responsibilities in a professional setting. I am confident that my positive attitude and willingness to learn will enable me to support the efficient operation of your stockroom.

I am particularly drawn to this role because I enjoy hands-on tasks and take pride in maintaining a tidy and organised environment. I understand the importance of keeping stockrooms orderly and ensuring that the inventory is accurately tracked and readily available when needed.

I am excited about the opportunity to contribute to Jamleys and gain valuable experience in the retail industry. I am available to work flexible hours and am eager to start as soon as possible.

Thank you for considering my application.

Your sincerely

A Jamieson

Alex Jamieson (They Them)

If you are a designer, though, you will need to steer clear of any ready-made templates like the ones pictured here. Anyone looking to employ a designer or artist, if presented with a creative covering letter, will expect the artwork and imagery within it to be the applicant's own work. If they spot that it's a pre-made template, they will be far from impressed, and before they even read your letter, it's likely to have been put in the rejection pile.

Applicant tracking systems (ATS)

In Chapter 5, we introduced you to applicant tracking systems (ATS). You may remember that it was stated that not all formats of letters are readable by some ATS. Prior to submitting your application, double-check it to make sure that, if it's being submitted via an ATS, it has been created in a format that can be read. If you have added design elements, some ATS won't recognise these or may jumble them up.

The ATS is most interested in reading the words in your letter and will totally ignore any graphic elements. Be careful not to put the text of your letter in a text box, as the ATS will consider anything in a text box to be a graphic and will ignore it. This is the last thing you want to happen, so avoid text boxes. You also need to ensure that any graphics you include do not contain words within them, especially keywords that are important to your application, because, unless they are repeated within the body of your letter, they might as well not be there if the ATS can't read them.

Unfortunately, and somewhat surprisingly, most ready-made templates on Word are not ATS-friendly as they are designed using numerous different boxes. These boxes will confuse the ATS, jumbling them up making your letter largely unreadable. Also, if you have created your letter using Pages, Google Docs, Illustrator or Canva, these too are unreadable to most ATS. Even if you export them and save them as PDFs, they will be graphic PDFs which the ATS cannot read.

By all means, add colour and graphics to your covering letter, but avoid text boxes and placing words within graphics, and remember to save as a Word doc or text PDF.

Of course, if you are planning to post or email your covering letter directly to a person, rather than submitting it online, the section relating to ATS won't apply to you.

IN A NUTSHELL

- Choose any colours and fonts carefully and thoughtfully to help communicate your personal brand.
- Keep it simple, consistent and authentic.
- Don't copy other people's creative ideas; use them as inspiration to showcase your own.
- Check to make sure your letter is ATS-compatible before submitting it.

11 TOP 10 COVERING LETTER WRITING MISTAKES TO AVOID

The first part of this book focuses on how to write your covering letter, where to start and what to include. You may have more experience in writing your letters and want a reminder of what not to include. Regardless of whether this is the first time you have written a covering letter or you have plenty of practice writing one, this chapter aims to remind you of the top 10 mistakes to avoid.

Use the checklist to make sure you don't make any of these mistakes:

☑ **Using the same covering letter for every application**

If you want to stand out from the crowd and give your application every chance, avoid falling into the trap of creating one covering letter and using it for 50 applications. You will not get shortlisted with this approach and probably won't even get a reply. Employers expect you to tailor your CV and covering letter to the job description, highlight your skills and experiences and explain why you are the ideal candidate for the role.

☑ Not doing any research

Doing your research is crucial. It is the backbone of your CV and covering letter. If you haven't taken time to reflect on yourself, that is, your skills and experiences, or the company, that is, its values or specialisms, how can you create a tailored covering letter? If you are unsure of how to start reflecting on your skills, look at Chapter 8 and the section on 'Speculative Letters', here you can find information on skills, terminology and a link to an activity to help you reflect on your skills.

☑ It's not all about YOU

While it is essential to sell your USP and outline to the employer why you are the best person for the job, remember this is a two-way process. Do not just focus on what you can get from the role. Outlining how your skills and experiences will benefit the company is equally important. This mistake links to no. 2, 'Not doing any research'. To be able to explain to an employer how you are the best fit, that is, due to your skills and experiences, and you are aligned with their values, you need to research this to be able to say it in your letter. If you need a reminder of what to research, look at Chapter 2, 'Understanding What Should Be in Each Section'.

☑ Strike the balance between formal/informal

When writing your covering letter, try to strike a balance between being too formal and too informal in your use of language. By researching the company you are applying to, you will get a sense of them as an employer, how their website and applications are written, and how formal they are. In addition, the type of sector you are applying to will help you understand what that sector expects, that is, law applications and letters tend to be more formal. Use this information to draft your covering letter to them. Do not be too informal, that is, Hi there or Hello, remember to use the right kind of introduction and greeting. If you are unsure how to start your letter, look at Chapter 2, 'Understanding What Should Be in Each Section'.

☑ Don't write war and peace

Like the section above, your letter needs to have just the right balance, and its length is important! If you write your letter over multiple pages, the employer will lose interest in your application. Most employers spend less than 10 minutes reviewing a CV and covering letter, and some acknowledge that they spend seconds on the process. You can't possibly tell your whole life story on a page. Remember, you want to create a one-page letter that is precise, to the point, and catches the employer's interest.

☑ Remember, attention to detail is important

It is important to check the details and not rely on using copy and paste because if you do, you are in danger of copying large chunks of text that might not be relevant or contain the wrong pronouns, that is, using 'he' instead of 'she' from a previous letter. Spend time editing the content of your letter and checking the details you have included. This is especially important if the application states they are looking for an applicant with attention to detail.

☑ Typos and spelling mistakes

Typos and spelling mistakes can impact the first impression of your covering letter. If it is a minor error or typo, the employer may overlook this, but if the errors continue throughout your letter, this could impact whether you are shortlisted. If grammar isn't your strong point, it's essential to be aware of this. You can use the spelling and grammar function on Microsoft Word. Try the Read Aloud function, which reads your words and can help you identify mistakes, or sign up for a free grammar software programme. In addition, print off your letter. Having the letter on paper in front of you can help you further identify errors. Proofreading is also important. Consider asking a friend, peer and so on to read through the letter to ensure no typos or grammatical errors.

☑ Make the most of your letter – don't copy your CV

The idea of your covering letter is to provide further information. It's not a copy; it is supposed to complement and work with your CV. As outlined in Chapter 2, you get the space to demonstrate to the employer how you meet the job specification and show some of your passion and interest in your chosen sector.

☑ Not following the instructions

Chapter 1 outlines when you should write a covering letter. It is essential to read the advert and check the application instructions. If the application says not to send a CV and covering letter and requests you complete the personal statement part of the application, then basically, it is a waste of your time writing a covering letter and vice versa. Check and double-check what the employer is asking for, and ensure you know what they want you to cover in the letter, that is, 'A cracking covering letter providing to us how good you are with words' (cgpbooks, 2023).

☑ Personalise, not personal

You want your letter to stand out from the crowd and for the employer to shortlist you for an interview. The above tips have outlined common mistakes. Throughout the book, we have given you the tools to write your letter without relying on someone else to write it for you. To write a compelling covering letter, you need to take all this knowledge and then add a touch of sparkle, personalising the letter is important too, add a bit of your personality, but don't fall into the trap of telling the employer your life story and making the letter overly personal. Striking the balance of this is essential.

12 HOW AND WHERE TO ACCESS SUPPORT

Throughout this book, the focus has been on enabling you to draft and write your own covering letter. However, you can also access help and support from careers professionals either based in or referred to by your school, college or university. They can help you with how to get started with your job search and provide you with support and advice for all aspects of your career journey, including your covering letter.

This chapter focuses on where to turn when you need that support, no matter where you are in your career journey, and will cover:

- job searching;

- advice and support when writing a covering letter;

- where to gain proofreading support.

This chapter will help you:

- have a better understanding of the types of support on offer;

- know whom to turn to when you need advice and support.

Job searching, support, advice and proofreading

If you're new to job searching, you may not know where to start, and that's okay. If you're applying for jobs and are unsure about the application process, for example, writing a covering letter, this chapter will outline some key places to gain some help, advice and support from your own institution.

School/academy

At your school, there will be a named careers leader or career adviser, depending on the size of your school, there may be a small number of other people who support the careers provision at your school. The careers leader should be your first point of contact. They will know what provision your school has, and they will also have links to a careers adviser and know what support exists externally. Make an appointment to speak with them, and they will be able to provide some initial advice and support on job searching, where to start and tell you what support is available in your school.

Further Education college

If you are based at a college or sixth form, you will usually find they have a careers support and guidance team. The size of the team will depend on your individual college, and it may be based in the student services area of your campus.

Information and advice are often provided by the broader team, that is, the employability and progression team. They are usually the first point of contact; they can help get you started and signpost you to a careers adviser.

Employability and progression team: offers information and advice; they may offer a quick query drop-in service.

Careers Adviser: offering face-to-face and/or online appointments, helping you with guidance interviews, that is, higher education guidance, mock interviews and employment interviews. They also provide appointments on employability and enterprise skills, placements and so on.

Information resources: in your careers area you will usually be able to access a careers library with information resources for you to look at. In addition, your college will also have online resources that you should be able to access remotely, whether you are on campus or not.

Many students don't realise what support is on offer for them from their careers team, so find out where they are based and pay them a visit. Make this a priority; the earlier you start to engage with the team, the more you will benefit and be ready for what is next on your career journey.

Higher Education: Careers and employment support

As a student or graduate of a university, your institution will have an array of support to offer to you.

Each university will have a careers team that offers career support. These teams usually have a broad focus, including careers resources, employability, student development and so on.

They will usually comprise several careers advisers or consultants. In most universities, each adviser will be aligned to a faculty.

Usually, you can arrange an appointment with any member of the team, but you can also arrange an appointment with the named contact for your faculty, that is, arts and humanities or engineering and physical sciences. Many teams will also have some advisers who have a specific specialism, for example, international or disability.

Careers Adviser/Consultant: offering one-to-one bookable appointments either online or in person, and may also offer drop-in sessions on specific days, between particular times. They will support you in a range of areas, for example, covering letters, CVs and applications, as well as advice and guidance on a wide range of employability areas.

In addition, as part of the careers team, there are usually several professionals who focus on employer engagement and/or work experience. They may also be aligned to specific faculties or have a central focus.

Employer engagement advisers: offering one-to-one bookable appointments either online or in person, and may also offer drop-in sessions on specific days. They will support you in exploring your job-searching strategy, how to job search, contact employers and so on.

Career fairs and employer events: Each year, your careers team will arrange a host of fairs and events. These include employer visits, panels, voluntary teaching, graduates' fairs and so on. Most of these events are face-to-face, but depending on your university, you may be able to access some online fairs.

Career workshops: Your university will offer a range of career workshops on topics, including transferable skills, networking, interview skills, writing covering letters and CVs and job searching.

Since Covid-19, your university may host more of its workshops online. They will probably be recorded and available as a resource you can go back to and watch as you have the time and space.

Online resources: You will also be able to access a range of resources via your university web page or portal. They may have a portal called CareersHub. This is the software that allows you to access your resources. You should be able to access this via your university systems; if you're a graduate, you may have to update your details, that is, email address and so on, so check. They will offer lots of career-related resources and tools, for example, job profiles, quizzes, support on how to write your CV and covering letter. You will be able to access an online job portal or something like Handshake, an early career network and career management platform connecting over 900 universities and 500,000 employers. Also, they have a 'meet the team' section, as well as a section about what they offer. You will also be able to access employers, events and a selection of other resources.

Make it your business to find out where the careers team is based on campus and visit. Many will have their area on campus; they will have a section of paper resources and be able to signpost you to the support they offer through both face-to-face and online resources and support.

Your careers team will probably not help with proofreading; however, they will identify some common mistakes in your CVs, covering letters and applications. At your university, you may well have access to support via your academic skills department. They may also review your CV, covering letter and so on, so it's best to make contact with your careers team and ask if this type of support is offered at your university.

Don't be the graduate who finishes their studies and never visits the careers team; this support is free for you, is tailored to you as a student and graduate and can help make all the difference when it comes to standing out from the crowd and getting that dream job.

If you feel unsure how your university careers service can help you as a student or graduate, contact your careers team and ask. However, for a further overview of why you should use their services, look at 'Further Reading and Resources'.

As a higher education careers adviser, the number of times I heard students say, 'I wish I'd known about this sooner' or 'you've been so helpful, I wish I had come to see you last year', is too numerous to mention. To be successful, students need to be proactive and seek out the support they need rather than expecting it to come to them. (J Hanley, HE Career Adviser)

IN A NUTSHELL

This chapter aims to be an introduction and/or a reminder of what support is on offer to you whether you are a student at school, college or university.

- Find out where your career leader and/or team are based.

- Go and visit the physical careers area, and access the online resources.

- Make an appointment with a careers adviser, even if you don't know what you want to do. They can help you get started.

13 IN A NUTSHELL

This chapter summarises some of the key factors from this book into a handy top 10 list of hints and tips. Following these should help ensure your covering letter is the best it can be.

1. Remember that your letter provides the space to explain in more depth how and why you are the best applicant for the role.

2. Check the application requirements, use the job specification as a checklist, do your research and remember the basic ingredients, that is, introduce yourself, why you and why them.

3. Tailor your letter to the relevant audience in mind, that is, graduate employer, and highlight your unique selling points, that is, transferable skills.

4. You are trying to convince the employer to invite you for an interview. Use the rule of three alongside power verbs to persuade rather than beg.

5. Using a speculative letter is a great way to access the hidden job market; however, doing your research and tailoring your letter is so important. If you're going to write a negotiation letter or a promotion letter, again, do your research, know your worth, and if you are resigning, do so on a positive note.

6. Disclosing personal information within a covering letter, most of the time, is a personal choice rather than a legal requirement. If you choose to do so, make sure it's done in a way that is relevant and within a sentence highlighting what you can bring to the role.

7. Always follow the instructions given by the employer on how to submit your CV and covering letter. If you have a choice, use the method that will help you stand out from the crowd in a positive way.

8. Choose any colours and fonts carefully and thoughtfully to help communicate your personal brand. But keep your letter simple, consistent and authentic.

9. Use the top 10 tips as a checklist, a reminder of what not to do when you are writing your covering letter.

10. While *You're Hired:, Compelling Covering Letters* aims to provide you with all the information, support and tips you will need to write your covering letter, remember there is support at your school, college or university. Don't leave it until you leave or graduate to seek out the support, advice and guidance from your careers team.

FURTHER READING AND RESOURCES

In each chapter of this book, we have covered a specific aspect of writing a covering letter, whether that be helping you understand what a cover letter is, in Chapter 1, 'What Is a Covering Letter?', to Chapter 10, 'Style and Substance'. In this chapter, we have collated sources of further reading and resources that you can use to assist you in writing a letter that will help you stand out from the crowd.

Chapter 1 – 'What Is a Covering Letter?' – explains what a covering letter is and why and when to write one. Below, you will find some further resources that can help explain this further.

- Indeed (2024) What Is a Cover Letter? (And What to Include in One) https://www.indeed.com/career-advice/resumes-cover -letters/what-is-a-cover-letter

- Indeed (2024) Things to Avoid When Writing a Cover Letter. https://www.indeed.com/career-advice/resumes-cover-letters/ what-not-to-put-in-a-cover-letter

- Prospects (2024) What Is a Cover Letter? https://www.prospects .ac.uk/careers-advice/cvs-and-cover-letters/cover-letters#what -is-a-cover-letter

- National Careers Service (2024) When to Include a Cover Letter. https://nationalcareers.service.gov.uk/careers-advice/covering -letter

Chapter 2 — 'Understanding What Should Be in Each Section'

— helps you understand what to include in your letter, that is, paragraph 1 is the introduction, and so on, as well as outline what to include in each paragraph and provide an example. Here, we've provided you with some activities and sources for further reading.

- World of Work (2023) Career Drivers: A Simple Introduction and Activity. https://worldofwork.io/2019/02/career-drivers-activity/

- Indeed: How to Write the Perfect Cover Letter. (https://uk .indeed.com/career-advice/cvs-cover-letters/the-perfect-cover -letter)

- National Careers Service: How to Write a Cover Letter. (https:// nationalcareers.service.gov.uk/careers-advice/covering-letter)

- Prospects. Cover Letters. (https://www.prospects.ac.uk/careers -advice/cvs-and-cover-letters/cover-letters)

- Manage your public profile URL | LinkedIn Help.

Chapter 3 — 'How to Tailor the Letter to the Job and Company'

— aims to help you to effectively tailor your covering letter to the specific company and job specification. It provides an example of a person specification and takes you through the steps to tailor your letter to the employer while reminding you about style and content.

- Glassdoor — Companies & reviews | Glassdoor

- Indeed — Find the best companies to work for | Indeed.com

- National Careers Service — Explore careers | National careers service

- Prospects — Job profiles | Prospects.ac.uk

- Target Jobs — Job descriptions: graduate careers advice | targetjobs

Chapter 4 – 'Words and Language' – explains why it is essential to understand the purpose of your letter, know your audience, explains the power to persuade and outlines power and keywords, and why you need to be concise. Here are a few additional resources you can use to help you explore this topic further.

- Eight Persuasive Writing Tips (With Helpful Examples) | Indeed .com

- How to Use the 'Rule of Three' to Create Engaging Content – Copyblogger

- BEG | English meaning – *Cambridge Dictionary*

Chapter 5 – 'The Use of AI with Covering Letters' – explains how to use generative AI to write a covering letter, the pros and cons of using AI and recognising applicant tracking systems. You might not be as aware of how to use AI, so we have provided a few more resources to help you.

- Level up your AI prompt writing for better covering letter drafts – CareerWise (ceric.ca)

- Employers reveal how AI is changing early careers recruitment | ISE Insights

Chapter 6 – 'One Size Doesn't Always Fit All' aims to help you realise why one size does not fit all, the importance of tailoring your letter and to consider your unique selling points depending on where you are in your career journey.

- www.prospects.ac.uk

- www.myworldofwork.co.uk

- www.nationalcareers.service.gov.uk

References:

- Zippa Average Number of Jobs in a Lifetime [2023]: How Many Jobs Does The Average Person Have — Zippia

- ONS UK job-to-job move rate 2023 | Statista

- ACAS hybrid working https://www.acas.org.uk/new-survey -shows-3-in-5-employers-have-seen-an-increase-in-hybrid -working-since-the-pandemic

- Five ways graduates feel about hybrid working | Luminate (prospects.ac.uk)

- Bath Spa University (2023). Guide to Using the STAR (R) Approach. Guide-to-Using-the-STAR-Approach.pdf (bathspa.ac .uk)

- The University of Edinburgh (2022) European Union Undergraduate Entry Requirements: Poland. https://www.ed.ac. uk/studying/international/european-union-undergraduate- entry-requirements/m-s/poland#:~:text=GCSEs%20are%20 a%20UK%20qualification%20typically%20taken%20 two,Level%20subject%20with%20the%20specified%20 equivalent%20grades%20below

- The University of Manchester (n.d.) Poland / Entry requirements. https://www.manchester.ac.uk/study/ international/country-specific-information/poland/ entry-requirements/

- Linguaholic (2023) How to Highlight Language Abilities on a Cover Letter. How to Highlight Language Abilities on a Cover Letter (linguaholic.com)

- https://www.linkedin.com/feed/update/urn:li:activity :7195815083489292288/

- National Foundation for Education Research (NFER) (2023) An analysis of the demand for skills in the labour market in 2035. Working paper 3: https://www.nfer.ac.uk/media/5360/the_skills _imperative_2035_working_paper_3_an_analysis_of_the _demand_for_skills_in_the_labour_market_in_2035.pdf

- Pearsons (2–17) The Future Demand for Skills in 2030. https://media.nesta.org.uk/documents/the_future_of_skills _employment_in_2030_0.pdf

Chapter 7 – 'Disclosing and Sharing Sensitive Information' – explores a range of topic areas, that is age, criminal convictions, disability, neurodivergence, sexual orientation and so on. It aims to help provide you with further insight and information for you to consider.

Age

- Equality and Human Rights Commission: Age discrimination

- Advisory, Conciliation and Arbitration Service: ACAS Guide on Age Discrimination

- Young Workers Loyal to Employers – But They Struggle Financially: New Survey – Pivotal Integrated HR Solutions (pivotalsolutions.com)

Caring responsibilities

- Carers Trust – Home – Carers Trust
- Carers UK – UK | Carers UK

Criminal convictions

- Unlock – Employment, Business and Volunteering – Unlock

- NACRO – Nacro | We See Your Future, Whatever The Past
- Check if you need to tell someone about your criminal record: Prison sentences – GOV.UK (www.gov.uk)

Disability

- Disclosing disability to an employer. https://www.scope.org.uk/advice-and-support/disclosing-disability-to-an-employer/
- Examples of how to disclose a disability in a covering letter. https://www.prospects.ac.uk/careers-advice/cvs-and-cover-letters/cover-letters/example-of-how-to-disclose-a-disability-in-a-cover-letter
- Example of how to disclose a disability in a covering letter | Prospects.ac.uk, CV Writing Tips
- British Deaf Association (bda.org.uk) A Deaf Person's Guide to Applying for Jobs | British Deaf News

Neurodivergence

- Two-thirds of workers won't disclose neurodiversity to bosses | IOSH
- AGCAS – disclosure.pdf (agcas.org.uk)
- National Autistic Society – Seeking work (autism.org.uk)

Gaps in work experience

- Indeed – How to explain job gaps (with a list of examples) | Indeed.com UK
- BBC – Are we done with the CV gap taboo? – BBC Worklife

Gender reassignment

- Equality and Human Rights Commission – Gender reassignment discrimination | EHRC (equalityhumanrights.com)
- Chartered Institute of Personnel and Development (CIPD) – Transgender and non-binary equality, diversity and inclusion in the workplace | CIPD

Sexual orientation

- TargetJobs – UK employment law, recruitment and the workplace: an explainer (targetjobs.co.uk)
- CIPD – Sexual orientation, gender identity and gender reassignment | CIPD
- Prospects.ac.uk – Getting a job as an LGBTQ+ graduate | Prospects.ac.uk

Religious beliefs

- Main Practiced Religions In The UK | UK Deed Poll Service
- Religion or belief discrimination | EHRC (equalityhumanrights .com)

Right to work in the UK

- Prospects.ac.uk – Work in the UK | Prospects.ac.uk

Chapter 8 – 'Other Ways of Using a Covering Letter' – in this chapter, we covered the other ways you can use your covering letter, that is, speculative application and so on. The chapter aims to help you understand what a speculative letter is, when and how to use one and how to create one, along with how to use and create the other letters. It also provides you with some templates. Here are some further resources that can help you.

- Prospects (2024). Job profiles. https://www.prospects.ac.uk/job-profiles

- National Careers Service (2024) Explore careers. https://nationalcareers.service.gov.uk/explore-careers

- Indeed (2023) What is the hidden job market? https://uk.indeed.com/career-advice/finding-a-job/hidden-job-market

- University of Surrey (n.d.) Job Seeking: The Hidden Job Market. https://www.surrey.ac.uk/sites/default/files/2018-10/job-seeking-the-hidden-job-market.pdf

- Prospects (2023) Speculative cover letter. https://www.prospects.ac.uk/careers-advice/cvs-and-cover-letters/cover-letters/speculative-cover-letter

- LinkedIn (2024) Creating a LinkedIn profile that opens doors. https://members.linkedin.com/en-gb/create-or-update-your-profile-on-linkedin

- University of Surrey (2023) Surrey Careers Blog How to find a job that isn't advertised. https://blogs.surrey.ac.uk/careers/2023/04/18/how-to-find-a-job-that-isnt-advertised/#:~:text=According%20to%20some%20estimates%2C%20up%20to%2080%25%20of,such%20as%20jobs%20boards%20or%20company%20career%20pages

- (12 Ways to Negotiate a Salary After the Job Offer (scienceofpeople.com))

- Salary guides: Reed https://www.reed.com/tools/uk-salary-guide-2024

- Hayes (2024) Latest Salary Guides and Trends – Access to Pay Guide Reports UK. https://www.hays.co.uk/salary-guide

- Milkround https://www.milkround.com/advice/how-to-negotiate-salary-in-the-uk

- ACAS (2022) Resignation notice letter template. https://www.acas.org.uk/resignation-letter-template

References:

- Indeed (2024) Pay bands in the UK. https://uk.indeed.com/hire/c/info/pay-bands-in-the-uk

- https://uk.indeed.com/career-advice/pay-salary/what-is-salary-band

- Science of People (2024) 20 Ways to Negotiate a Salary After the Job Offer. 20 Ways to Negotiate a Salary After the Job Offer (scienceofpeople.com)

Chapter 9 – 'Digital versus Paper Letters' – aims to give you some further insight into the pros and cons of using electronic versus paper correspondence; provides some further insights into layouts, addresses, pronouns and so on, so no matter which format you are applying through, you know what is expected. You can have a look at some further information via the resources below.

- Top CV – Best file formats for CV: guide to choosing the right one | TopCV

- Grammarly – 6 Tips for Formatting a Cover Letter, With Examples | Grammarly

References:

- The economic impact of digital inclusion in the UK, 2022

Chapter 10 – 'Style and Substance' – aims to help you think about adding design elements, branding, and being authentic, and provided some examples of creative covering letters. It introduced you to applicant tracking systems (ATS) and what to be mindful of when writing your applications.

- A guide to colour meaning | Adobe
- The definition of font psychology and how to use it (canva.com)

Chapter 11 – 'Top 10 Covering Letter Writing Mistakes to Avoid' – collated the top mistakes that have been outlined throughout the book and brought them together to give you a checklist and an accessible reminder of what not to do when writing your covering letter.

Chapter 12 – 'How and Where to Access Support' – provides an overview of where you can get support, whether you are at a school, college or university. It provides a brief overview of the type of support you may be able to access, no matter where you are on your career journey.

- Why use your university careers service? Why use your university careers service? | Prospects.ac.uk

Chapter 13 – 'In a Nutshell' – summarises some of the key factors from this book into a handy top 10 list of hints and tips. Following these should help ensure your covering letter is the best it can be.

THE 'YOU'RE HIRED' SERIES

These essential guides for job hunters show how to research, apply for and land the dream job. Each book is written by a careers professional and provides:

- ✓ Specialist advice to help students in their job search
- ✓ Practical exercises to boost confidence and improve performance
- ✓ Insider tips from experts

Estd. 1969 **trotman** t

For more information
and to buy, visit:
https://trotman.co.uk/products/youre-hired-series-pack

www.ingramcontent.com/pod-product-compliance
Lightning Source LLC
Chambersburg PA
CBHW041145230326
41599CB00039BA/7179